3/23

P9-CKO-488

What People Are Saying About Our Books

*"Trusting a recipe often comes down to trusting the source.
The sources for the recipes are impeccable;
in fact, they're some of the best chefs in the nation."*
BON APPÉTIT MAGAZINE

"Should be in the library — and kitchen — of every serious cook."
JIM WOOD — Food & Wine Editor — San Francisco Examiner

*"A well-organized and user-friendly tribute to many of the states'
finest restaurant chefs."*
SAN FRANCISCO CHRONICLE

*"An attractive guide to the best restaurants and inns,
offering recipes from their delectable repertoire of menus."*
GAIL RUDDER KENT — Country Inns Magazine

"Outstanding cookbook"
HERITAGE NEWSPAPERS

*"I couldn't decide whether to reach for my telephone and make reservations
or reach for my apron and start cooking."*
JAMES MCNAIR — Best-selling cookbook author

"It's an answer to what to eat, where to eat — and how to do it yourself."
THE HERALD

*"I dare you to browse through these recipes
without being tempted to rush to the kitchen."*
PAT GRIFFITH — Chief, Washington Bureau, Blade Communications, Inc.

Books of the "Secrets" Series

FLORIDA'S

GUIDEBOOK & COOKBOOK

COOKING SECRETS

Kathleen DeVanna Fish

BON
VIVANT

All rights reserved. No portion of this book may be reproduced or transmitted in any form or by any means, electronic or mechanical, including photocopying, without permission in writing from the publisher, except for the inclusion of brief quotations in a review.

Library of Congress Cataloguing-in-Publication Data

FLORIDA'S COOKING SECRETS
The Chefs' Secret Recipes

First printing, 1998

Fish, Kathleen DeVanna
97-073976
ISBN 1-883214-19-X
$15.95 softcover
Includes indexes
Autobiography page

Copyright © 1998 by Kathleen DeVanna Fish
Cover photography by Robert N. Fish
Cover design by Abalone Design Group
Editorial direction by Judie Marks
Editorial assistance by Nadine Guarrera
Illustrations by Krishna Gopa
Type by Cimarron Design

Published by Bon Vivant Press
an imprint of The Millennium Publishing Group
P.O. Box 1994
Monterey, CA 93942

Printed in the United States of America
by Banta Book Group

Contents

Florida Restaurants and Inns

Keys

Southern

Central

Northern

Chef's Favorite Recipes

Breakfast and Breads

Appetizers

Soups

Salads and Dressings

Game and Poultry

Chestnut-Crusted Chicken Breast with Black Truffle Sauce—**Il Tartufo on Las Olas,** *99*

Chili Spiced Quail with Kahlúa Orange Sauce—**Café Arugula,** *37*

Chicken alla Cacciatore—**Belleview Mido Resort Hotel,** *198*

Boundary Waters Stuffed Chicken—**Chesterfield Hotel,** *120*

Chicken Breast with Balsamic Vinegar—
Royal Palm House Bed and Breakfast, *147*

Florida Citrus Mojo Turkey—**Boca Raton Resort and Club,** *117*

Chicken Scarpedella—**Top of Daytona,** *246*

Meat

Marinated Lamb—**Chez Pierre,** *233*

Costoletta di Maiale—**Portobello Yacht Club,** *192*

Baby Lamb Chops with Mashed Potatoes, Spinach and Balsamic Sauce—
Pelican Hotel, *138*

Leg of Lamb in Puff Pastry—**Bijou Café,** *159*

Goat Cheese-Crusted Rack of Lamb—**St. George and the Dragon,** *108*

Steak Fromage—**Fifth Avenue Grill,** *91*

Fire Licked Skirt Steak—**Barracuda Grill,** *31*

Garlic Stuffed Tenderloin of Beef—**Grove Isle Club and Resort,** *125*

Ossobuco alla Milanese—**Belleview Mido Resort Hotel,** *197*

Grilled Pork Tenderloin with Beet Vinaigrette—**Top of Daytona,** *245*

Veal Chops alla Senese—**Antonio's La Fiamma,** *155*

Honey Chile Glazed Pork Chop—**Café Arugula,** *38*

Filet Mignon Toscano—**Amici,** *69*

Barcelona Stir-Fry—**Café Tu Tu Tango,** *170*

Seafood

Pasta and Grains

Sauces and Condiments

Final Temptations

Catalan Custard—**Café Seville**, *77*

Warm Sauté of Summer Fruit—**Bijou Café**, *160*

White Chocolate Spice Ice Cream with Mango-Vanilla Compote and Tropical Fruit Salsa—**Cheeca Lodge**, *49*

White Chocolate Mousse with Oreo Cookie Crust—**California Café Bar and Grill**, *81*

Red Wine Poached Pears—**Chez Pierre**, *235*

Key Lime Pie—**Fulton's Crab House**, *175*

Grand Marnier Soufflé—**Park Plaza Gardens**, *187*

Mango "Tarte Tatin" with Banana Ice Cream and Kumquat Aspic—**Grand Cafe**, *94*

Sesame-Crusted Angelic Drunken Peach Trifle—**Damiano's at the Tarrimore House**, *86*

Tiramisu—**Top of Daytona**, *247*

Orange-Berry Zabaglione—**Café Arugula**, *39*

Cooking Stars of Florida

AMICI

ITALIAN CUISINE
288 SOUTH COUNTY ROAD
PALM BEACH, FLORIDA 33480
(561)832-0201
Page 66

ANTONIO'S LA FIAMMA

ITALIAN CUISINE
611 SOUTH ORLANDO AVENUE
MAITLAND, FLORIDA
(407) 645-5523
Page 152

BAGATELLE

TROPICAL CUISINE
115 DUVAL STREET
KEY WEST, FLORIDA 33040
(305) 296-6609
Page 24

BARRACUDA GRILL

SEAFOOD CUISINE
MILE MARKER 49.5
4290 OVERSEAS HIGHWAY
MARATHON, FLORIDA 33050
(305) 743-3314
Page 28

BIJOU CAFÉ

CONTINENTAL CUISINE
1287 FIRST STREET
SARASOTA, FLORIDA 34236
(941) 366-8111
Page 156

THE BISTRO

CONTINENTAL CUISINE
2611 PONCE DE LEON BOULEVARD
CORAL GABLES, FLORIDA 33134
(305) 442-9671
Page 70

CAFÉ ARUGULA

"CUISINES OF THE SUN"
3150 NORTH FEDERAL HIGHWAY
LIGHTHOUSE POINT, FLORIDA 33064
(954) 785-7732
Page 32

CAFÉ CREOLE AND OYSTER BAR

CAJUN AND CREOLE CUISINE
1330 EAST NINTH AVENUE
YBOR CITY, FLORIDA 33605
(813) 247-6283
Page 162

CAFÉ C'RIZMA

CONTEMPORARY AMERICAN CUISINE

3218 SOUTH ATLANTIC AVENUE

DAYTONA BEACH SHORES, FLORIDA 32118

(904) 767-3080

Page 226

CAFÉ SEVILLE

SPANISH CUISINE

2768 EAST OAKLAND BOULEVARD

FORT LAUDERDALE, FLORIDA 33306

(954) 565-1148

Page 74

CAFÉ TU TU TANGO

ECLECTIC "APPETIZER" CUISINE

8625 INTERNATIONAL DRIVE

ORLANDO, FLORIDA 32819

(407) 248-2222

Page 168

CALIFORNIA CAFÉ BAR AND GRILL

CALIFORNIA AND
MEDITERRANEAN CUISINE

2301 SOUTHEAST 17TH STREET CAUSEWAY

FORT LAUDERDALE, FLORIDA 33316

(954) 728-3500

Page 78

CHEZ PIERRE

FRENCH CUISINE
1215 THOMASVILLE ROAD
TALLAHASSEE, FLORIDA 32303
(850) 222-0936
Page 232

DAMIANO'S AT THE TARRIMORE HOUSE

TRANSCONTINENTAL AND
FLORASIAN CUISINE
52 NORTH SWINTON
DELRAY BEACH, FLORIDA 33447
(407) 272-4706
Page 82

FIFTH AVENUE GRILL

STEAKHOUSE AND TRADITIONAL
AMERICAN CUISINE
821 SOUTHEAST 5TH AVENUE
DELRAY BEACH, FLORIDA 33483
(561) 265-0122
Page 88

FULTON'S CRAB HOUSE

SEAFOOD CUISINE
PLEASURE ISLAND
1670 BUENA VISTA DRIVE
LAKE BUENA VISTA, FLORIDA 32802
(407) 934-2628
Page 172

GRAND CAFE

NEW FLORIDA CUISINE
2669 SOUTH BAYSHORE DRIVE
COCONUT GROVE, FLORIDA
(305) 858-9600
Page 92

IL TARTUFO ON LAS OLAS

CONTINENTAL CUISINE
2400 EAST LAS OLAS BOULEVARD
FORT LAUDERDALE, FLORIDA 33301
(954) 767-9190
Page 96

JAMIE'S FRENCH RESTAURANT

FRENCH CUISINE
424 EAST ZARRAGOSSA
PENSACOLA, FLORIDA 32501
(850) 434-2911
Page 236

MAISON AND JARDIN

CONTINENTAL CUISINE
430 SOUTH WYMORE ROAD
ALTAMONTE SPRINGS, FLORIDA 32714
(407) 862-4410
Page 176

MANGIA MANGIA

ITALIAN CUISINE
900 SOUTHARD STREET
KEY WEST, FLORIDA 33040
(305) 294-2469
Page 40

NORMAN'S

NEW WORLD CUISINE
21 ALMERIA AVENUE
CORAL GABLES, FLORIDA 33134
(305) 446-6767
Page 100

PARK PLAZA GARDENS

CONTEMPORARY AMERICAN CUISINE
319 PARK AVENUE SOUTH
WINTER PARK, FLORIDA 32789
(407) 645-2475
Page 182

PORTOBELLO YACHT CLUB

NORTHERN ITALIAN CUISINE
PLEASURE ISLAND
1650 BUENA VISTA DRIVE
LAKE BUENA VISTA, FLORIDA 32802
(407) 934-8888
Page 188

ST. GEORGE AND THE DRAGON

CONTINENTAL CUISINE

936 FIFTH AVENUE SOUTH

NAPLES, FLORIDA 34102

(941) 262-6546

Page 106

SOVEREIGN

CONTINENTAL CUISINE

12 SOUTHEAST SECOND AVENUE

GAINESVILLE, FLORIDA 32601

(352) 378-6307

Page 240

TOP OF DAYTONA

FRENCH AND ITALIAN CUISINE

2625 SOUTH ATLANTIC AVENUE

DAYTONA BEACH SHORES, FLORIDA 32118

(904) 767-5791

Page 244

VITO'S WATERFRONT

ITALIAN CUISINE

1079 BALD EAGLE DRIVE

MARCO ISLAND, FLORIDA 34145

(941) 394-7722

Page 110

BAGATELLE

TROPICAL CUISINE
115 Duval Street
Key West, Florida 33040
(305) 296-6609
Lunch Daily 11:30AM–3PM
Dinner Daily 5:30PM–10PM
Average Dinner for Two: $55

Bagatelle, "an Island Restaurant," has built a national reputation by combining its French heritage with the indigenous tastes of the tropics. Here, the chef blends the best of locally caught fresh seafood, fresh produce and delicious tropical fruit with the tradition of the classical French cuisine.

The restaurant has maintained the historic charm and architectural detail of its original gray-and-pink Queen Anne building. The second-story verandahs were designed to take advantage of Key West's tropical breezes while offering a bird's-eye view of Duval Street.

Luncheon highlights include Blackened Chicken Breast Sandwich with Crumbled Bleu Cheese, as well as a variety of Grilled Fish. Entrée favorites are the Snapper Macadamia with Mango Butter Sauce, the Garlic-Herb Pasta topped with Gulf Shrimp, the Bahamian Conch Steak and the Seared Tuna Rolled in Black Peppercorns. Delightful chicken and beef dishes are given a tropical treatment. Save room for the Stone Crab Cakes with Avocado Aioli and the Macadamia Banana Cream Pie.

BAGATELLE'S MENU FOR FOUR:

Tuna Tataki

Black Bean and Tasso Ham Soup

Conch Ceviche

Tuna Tataki

For the sauce: In the bowl of a food processor or in a mixing bowl, combine the ginger, soy sauce, garlic, rice wine vinegar and five-spice powder. Slowly drizzle in the peanut oil and sesame oil to emulsify.

For the pickled ginger: Place all of the ingredients in a small saucepan and cook together for 2 hours over low heat. Cool the ginger in the cooking liquid. Once cooled, separate the ginger from the liquid and reserve the cooking liquid for later use.

For the tuna: Roll the tuna loin in the freshly cracked black pepper. Sear the tuna on all sides in an extremely hot, dry skillet. Slice into very thin strips.

To serve, place ¼ cup of the sauce onto each of 4 plates and top each plate with slices of the tuna. Divide the pickled ginger into 4 portions and arrange attractively on the plates. Top each serving with toasted sesame seeds.

© Bagatelle, The Cookbook
Serves 4
Preparation Time:
  25 Minutes
(note marinating time)

½ Tbsp. fresh ginger, grated
¼ cup soy sauce
1 tsp. garlic, chopped
2 Tbsps. rice wine vinegar
Pinch of Chinese five-spice powder
¾ cup peanut oil
¼ cup sesame oil

Pickled Ginger:

¼ cup fresh ginger, peeled, thinly sliced
2 medium beets, coarsely chopped
3 cups red wine vinegar
1 cup rice wine vinegar

Tuna:

10 oz. fresh tuna loin
½ cup black peppercorns, very coarsely ground
1½ tsps. sesame seeds, toasted

Black Bean and Tasso Ham Soup

© Bagatelle, The Cookbook
Serves 4
Preparation Time:
  1½ Hours
(note soaking time)

  2 cups black beans or
    turtle beans
3½ qts. water
  ½ cup soy sauce
  ½ cup red wine vinegar
  ⅛ cup lime juice
  ½ cup Worcestershire
    sauce
  2 Tbsps. whole butter
  2 cups tasso ham, cut
    into ½-inch cubes
  ¾ cup red onion, diced
  2 Tbsps. garlic, chopped
  3 Tbsps. fresh rosemary,
    chopped
  ½ cup red bell pepper,
    diced
  ½ cup green bell pepper,
    diced
  ½ cup yellow bell pepper,
    diced
  1 tsp. cayenne pepper
  3 bay leaves
  ¼ cup sherry
  ¼ cup sour cream for
    garnish
  4 Tbsps. scallions,
    chopped, for garnish

Combine the beans with 1½ qts. water, soy sauce, red wine vinegar, lime juice and Worcestershire sauce in a ceramic or stainless steel bowl. Soak mixture overnight.

Place the butter, tasso ham, onion, garlic and rosemary in a stock pot and cook over medium-low heat for 5 minutes. Turn the heat up to high and add the peppers, cayenne, bay leaves and sherry.

Add the drained beans to the stock pot. Add the remaining water and simmer for 1 hour.

Remove 2 cups of beans from the soup and purée in a food processor or blender. Stir the purée back into the soup and simmer for 10 more minutes.

Garnish each bowl of soup with 1 Tbsp. of sour cream and chopped scallions.

☆

Conch Ceviche

ombine all of the above ingredients in a mixing bowl and let marinate, refrigerated, for a minimum of 3 hours.

Divide onto 4 plates and garnish with lime wedges and sprigs of cilantro.

© Bagatelle, The Cookbook
Serves 4
Preparation Time:
  15 Minutes
(note marinating time)

  1 lb. frozen conch steak, thinly sliced
  3 Tbsps. red bell pepper, diced
  3 Tbsps. green bell pepper, diced
  3 Tbsps. yellow bell pepper, diced
  4 Tbsps. red onion, diced
  1 scallion, diced
  ¼ bunch fresh cilantro
  1 cup lime juice
  ½ cup red wine vinegar
  ⅛ tsp. Scotch bonnet chile
  2 dashes Tabasco Sauce
  ½ tsp. salt
  1 tsp. ground white pepper
  3 Tbsps. olive oil
  4 lime wedges for garnish
  4 cilantro sprigs for garnish

☆

BARRACUDA GRILL

SEAFOOD CUISINE
Mile Marker 49.5
4290 Overseas Highway
Marathon, Florida 33050
(305) 743-3314
Dinner Monday–Saturday 6:30PM–10PM
Average Dinner for Two: $60

I n the middle of fried-fish eateries, there is the Barracuda Grill—an oasis of fine dining with all the attention to detail, elegance and passion associated with fashionable bistros in uptown restaurants.

Opened in 1994, chef-owners Jan and Lance Hill offer elegant creations emanating from their kitchen. Where else will you find Pepper Jelly-Glazed Grilled Beef Tenderloin next to Japanese Seaweed and Teriyaki Snapper on the menu. Other menu highlights are the Really Red Hot Calamari, painfully hot, intensely garlicky and just plain dangerous. The White Conch Chowder is made to order and loaded with tender conch, fresh cream, just-shucked corn and scallions and the Good Ole Shrimp Scampi with Sweet Pinks over Linguine with Lobster Butter, Garlic, White Wine, Parsley and Key Limes.

BARRACUDA GRILL'S MENU FOR TWO:

Really Red Hot Calamari

White Conch Chowder

Fire-Licked Skirt Steak

Really Red Hot Calamari

Mix together the butter, lobster base, black pepper, Key lime juice and garlic. Set aside.

Heat a sauté pan. Add the sesame seeds, hot sauce, white wine, scallions and lobster butter from above. Stir constantly while cooking. Add the calamari and cook until opaque. Be careful not to overcook.

Serves 2
Preparation Time:
  20 Minutes

  1 lb. butter, softened
  2 Tbsps. lobster base
  ½ Tbsp. black pepper
  2 Tbsps. Key lime juice
  2 Tbsps. garlic, puréed
  2 Tbsps. sesame seeds
  ⅓ cup hot sauce of your choice
  ¼ cup white wine
  ¼ cup scallions, sliced
  ½ lb. calamari, sliced into rings

☆

White Conch Chowder

Serves 2
Preparation Time:
  15 Minutes

1½ **cups heavy cream**
  4 **oz. conch, ground**
  1 **scallion, sliced**
  ¼ **cup corn, cut from the**
     cob
     Salt and pepper to
     taste

reheat a sauté pan over medium heat and add the cream, conch, scallion and corn. Reduce the cream until it starts to thicken.

Season to taste with salt and pepper and serve immediately.

☆

Fire-Licked Skirt Steak

Combine the balsamic vinegar, tamari, Worcestershire sauce, garlic, black pepper, hot sauce and cilantro in a blender. Blend together for a few seconds and then add the olive oil and blend for 45 seconds.

Marinate the skirt steak in the oil mixture for 4 hours, refrigerated.

Slice the skirt steak into sections approximately 6 inches long and submerse in the marinade for the time it takes to get your grill to the red-hot stage.

Grill meat on each side for 2 to 3 minutes. Because this cut of meat is rather thin, a very hot grill is required to sear the outside quickly while allowing the interior to remain rare.

Allow the skirt steak to rest in a warm place for 3 to 4 minutes. Slice against the grain, pile it high and drizzle with the natural juices that accumulated while it rested.

Serves 4 to 6
Preparation Time:
 30 Minutes
(note marinating time)

 ¾ **cup balsamic vinegar**
 ¾ **cup tamari**
 ½ **cup Worcestershire**
    sauce
 ¼ **cup garlic, puréed**
 ¼ **cup black pepper**
    Dash of hot sauce of
    your choice
 1 **bunch fresh cilantro**
1½ **cups olive oil**
 2 **to 3 lbs. skirt steak,**
    trimmed

☆

CAFÉ ARUGULA

"CUISINES OF THE SUN"
3150 North Federal Highway
Lighthouse Point, Florida 33064
(954) 785-7732
Dinner Sunday–Thursday 5:30PM–10PM
Dinner Friday and Saturday 5:30PM–10:30PM
Average Dinner for Two: $80

L egend has it owner Dick Cingolani became a chef when he opened his first restaurant and the chef didn't show up. It was then that Dick realized the only person to wear the hat was himself. His hobby became a lifelong career.

As a youth, he spent time in the kitchen learning to cook Italian cuisine, and later taught himself regional dishes from France, China and the Southwest by watching and reading the masters—Julia Child and Joyce Chen. Over the years his cooking styles have evolved into a fusion cuisine that he calls "cuisines of the sun."

Café Arugula's eclectic menu features Thai Shrimp Tacos, Moroccan Marinated Yellowfin Tuna, Cinnamon-Skewered Grilled Tandoori Pork, Wild Mushroom and Caramelized Onion-Crusted Steaks and a Banana-Rum Pecan Praline Tapioca Pudding.

CAFÉ ARUGULA'S MENU FOR SIX:

Santa Fe Sushi on Charred Tomato Sauce

Arugula Salad

Veal and Chicken Cannelloni

Chile Spiced Quail with Kahlúa Orange Sauce

Honey-Chile-Glazed Pork Chops

Orange-Berry Zabaglione

Santa Fe Sushi on Charred Tomato Sauce

Purée the cooked beans in a food processor to make a thick paste, adding some of the reserved liquid as necessary. Add the cilantro, cumin, jalapeño and salt to taste. Set aside.

Season chicken strips with salt and pepper and grill on the barbecue, or broil, until done.

Stir-fry or lightly steam spinach and cool.

Blanch the peppers and carrot for 2 minutes, then plunge into ice water.

Cut the jack and colby cheeses into long strips.

Lightly rub oil over the tortillas and place each in a hot skillet for 1 to 2 seconds, just to soften. Remove from pan and spread the black bean purée over the bottom third, about ¼-inch thick. Top with chicken strips in a line, end to end. Place a line of cheese on each side, top with a little spinach and a row of blanched vegetables.

Start at the full end and roll evenly and firmly, rubbing a little butter on the end to act as a glue to hold it all together.

Wrap in plastic and refrigerate at least one hour to firm up.

To serve, slice into 1-inch pieces and place cut side up, to look like sushi. Serve at room temperature over warm Charred Tomato Sauce.

Cooking Secret: This recipe, named the best appetizer recipe by the Miami Herald a few years ago, can be made ahead and refrigerated for up to two days.

© Café Arugula's
  Cuisines of the Sun Cookbook
Serves 6 to 8
Preparation Time:
  30 Minutes
(note refrigeration time)

  3 cups black beans, cooked (reserve some liquid)
  2 Tbsps. cilantro, chopped
  1 Tbsp. cumin, ground
  1 fresh jalapeño, diced
    Salt and pepper to taste
  ¾ lb. chicken, boneless, skinless, cut into ½-inch strips
  1 lb. fresh spinach
  1 red bell pepper, julienned
  1 yellow bell pepper, julienned
  1 carrot, julienned
  ½ lb. jalapeño jack cheese
  ½ lb. colby or cheddar cheese
  ½ cup vegetable oil
  6 10-inch flour tortillas
  1 Tbsp. soft butter
    Charred Tomato Sauce (recipe follows)

★

Charred Tomato Sauce

© *Café Arugula's*
  Cuisines of the Sun Cookbook
Yield: 4 cups
Preparation Time:
  15 Minutes

4 **medium ripe tomatoes**
1 **medium red onion,**
  peeled, quartered
4 **cloves garlic**
1 **chipotle chile or to**
  taste
¼ **cup cilantro, chopped**
  Salt and pepper to
  taste

P reheat a cast iron skillet until hot. Place the tomatoes, onion and garlic cloves in it. Char the skins black.

When all the vegetables have been charred, remove and scrape up all the charred skin and burnt particles. Peel the garlic. Core but do not peel the tomatoes.

Place in the bowl of a food processor. Add the remaining ingredients and purée to a chunky sauce. Adjust seasonings to your taste. Add more chipotle if you really like hot food.

Arugula Salad

Wash the arugula well. Unless you are able to get baby organic or hydroponic greens, they can be very sandy. Do not tear the leaves; they should be served whole. Add the Balsamic Dressing to the arugula and toss well.

To serve, place three endive leaves on the bottom of the plate, like spokes, and place a piece of sun-dried tomato on each leaf. In the center of the plate, pile up the arugula, sprinkle with the hazelnuts and then top with 3 or 4 good-sized shavings of Parmigiano-Reggiano. Serve immediately.

For the dressing: Place vinegar and seasonings in a bowl and slowly whisk in the olive oils until blended. It is easier to prepare this dressing in a food processor or mixer and it results in a smoother dressing. Refrigerate what you do not use; it will last for weeks. Don't worry if it gets thick and cloudy—just bring the dressing back to room temperature and it will clear.

© *Café Arugula's*
  Cuisines of the Sun Cookbook
Serves 4
Preparation Time:
  25 Minutes

  3 to 4 bunches arugula
  1 cup Balsamic Dressing
    (recipe follows)
  18 spears of Belgian
    endive
  18 sun-dried tomato
    pieces in oil
  ½ cup hazelnuts, toasted,
    skinned
    Parmigiano-Reggiano
    cheese to taste

Balsamic Dressing:
Yield: 3 cups

  ½ cup balsamic vinegar
  1 Tbsp. fresh rosemary,
    chopped
  1 Tbsp. garlic, chopped
  1 tsp. salt
  1 tsp. pepper
  2 cups olive oil
  2 cups extra virgin olive
    oil

Veal and Chicken Cannelloni

© *Café Arugula's*
  Cuisines of the Sun Cookbook
Yield: 12 cannelloni
Preparation Time:
  45 Minutes
Preheat oven to 350°

½ lb. chicken breast,
  boneless, skinless,
  ground
½ lb. veal, ground
2 Tbsps. olive oil
1 Tbsp. garlic, chopped
½ lb. spinach
1½ cups Béchamel Sauce
  (recipe follows)
¾ cup fresh Parmigiano-
  Reggiano, grated
  Salt and pepper to
  taste
1 lb. pasta, cooked and
  drained
2 cups tomato sauce
  Basil leaves for garnish,
  optional

Béchamel Sauce:

½ stick butter
¼ cup flour
2 cups milk
  Nutmeg to taste
  Salt and pepper to
  taste
½ cup fresh Parmigiano,
  grated

Sauté the chicken and veal in olive oil for about 5 minutes or until cooked. It will be grayish in color, not brown. Remove from the pan and drain the fat.

Sauté the garlic in the sauté pan, adding more olive oil if necessary, then add the spinach and stir-fry 1 or 2 minutes until wilted. Remove and chop coarsely, then add to the cooked meat. Mix in ¾ cups Béchamel Sauce, cheese, salt and pepper to taste. Cool.

Use blanched fresh pasta squares, large shells or large pasta tubes sold for stuffing. Stuff each shell with 2 to 3 Tbsps. filling. Place a little tomato sauce on the bottom of a baking pan big enough to hold all the cannelloni, and put them in the pan so they are almost touching, side by side. When the pan is full, cover the ends of the cannelloni with the tomato sauce and then spoon the remaining Béchamel Sauce down the middle.

Bake in a 350° oven for 25 minutes to heat through and blend the flavors. If the top starts to brown, cover it with foil. Serve garnished with fresh basil leaves.

For the béchamel sauce: Melt the butter. Add flour, stirring to blend well. Add milk all at once and whisk well. Bring to a boil, stirring with a whisk. Add seasonings and cheese, adding more milk if sauce is too thick.

☆

Chile Spiced Quail with Kahlúa Orange Sauce

For the rub mixture, toast the peppercorns, cumin, cinnamon, mustard and coriander seeds in a sauté pan until almost smoking. Purée in a coffee grinder or spice grinder with the bay leaf, dried chile, cayenne powder and espresso. Mix the rub spices well. Set aside.

Place the quail, breast side down, on a flat surface. With a pair of poultry shears, split the bird lengthwise, along the backbone. Open it flat and press down with the heel of your hand to flatten it completely. Cut down the backbone of each bird and flatten with the palm of your hand. Rub the spice mixture over the quail, allowing the birds to marinate for at least 30 minutes, refrigerated.

Sauté the quail in the olive oil and butter until golden brown. Using tongs so you don't pierce the meat, turn and cook the other side, about 15 minutes total cooking time. When the quail is almost cooked, glaze with a little Kahlúa.

Serve with Kahlúa Orange Sauce.

For the sauce: Sauté the garlic and shallots in butter in a sauté pan over medium heat. Add the stock, Kahlúa and cream. Bring mixture to a boil and reduce until thick. Add the remaining flavorings and cook for 2 minutes more.

© *Café Arugula's Cuisines of the Sun Cookbook*

Serves 6
Preparation Time:
  45 Minutes
(note marinating time)

  8 peppercorns
12 cumin seeds
  1 cinnamon stick
  8 mustard seeds
  8 coriander seeds
  1 bay leaf
  1 dried ancho chile
  ½ tsp. cayenne powder
  ½ cup instant espresso, finely ground
  6 quail hens
  2 Tbsps. olive oil
  2 Tbsps. butter
    Splash of Kahlúa

Kahlúa Orange Sauce:

  1 Tbsp. garlic, chopped
  2 Tbsps. shallots, chopped
  3 Tbsps. butter
  3 cups chicken stock
  1 cup Kahlúa
  ½ cup heavy cream
  1 tsp. vanilla
  2 Tbsps. orange zest
  ½ cup orange juice
    Salt and pepper to taste

Honey-Chile-Glazed Pork Chops

© Café Arugula's
Cuisines of the Sun Cookbook
Serves 6
Preparation Time:
  45 Minutes
(note steeping time)
Preheat oven to 400°

  1 **medium onion, diced**
  2 **Tbsps. olive oil**
  ½ **Scotch bonnet chile,**
    seeded, diced fine
  2 **dried ancho or pasilla**
    chiles, julienned
  2 **cups orange blossom**
    honey
  ½ **cup cilantro, chopped**
  6 **pork chops**

Sauté the onion in olive oil over medium heat until golden brown.

Add the chiles and cook 1 minute.

Add the honey and bring to a boil. Reduce the heat and simmer for 5 minutes. Remove from heat and let steep together for at least 1 hour. Add the cilantro. Set aside.

Grill or sauté the chops to brown, about 2 minutes per side. Glaze by brushing on honey-chile glaze and bake in a 400° oven until the interior temperature of the chops is 150°, about 10 minutes.

Glaze chops again and let rest before serving.

Orange-Berry Zabaglione

Beat the yolks and sugar in a stainless steel bowl until the mixture is thick and the sugar is mixed well, about 2 minutes.

Place the bowl over a pot of boiling water to act as a double boiler.

Add the orange juice and cook gently over low heat, whisking constantly until thick and fluffy. Be careful not to let the simmering water touch the bottom of the bowl, or you could scramble the egg mixture.

Add the Grand Marnier; remove from the heat and let cool.

Whip the cream with the powdered sugar until stiff, then fold into the cooled egg mixture.

To serve, place the berries in a decorative glass and spoon or pour zabaglione mixture over the fruit. Garnish with mint.

Cooking Secret: Zabaglione can be served warm or refrigerated for up to 3 days.

© *Café Arugula's*
   Cuisines of the Sun Cookbook
Serves 6 to 8
Preparation Time:
   30 Minutes

4 **egg yolks**
½ **cup sugar**
½ **cup orange or**
   tangerine juice
½ **cup Grand Marnier or**
   champagne
1 **cup heavy cream**
2 **Tbsps. powdered sugar**
3 **pts. of berries:**
   raspberries,
   strawberries or a
   combination of berries
   Mint for garnish

☆

MANGIA MANGIA

ITALIAN CUISINE
900 Southard Street
Key West, Florida 33040
(305) 294-2469
Daily 5:30PM–10PM
Average Dinner For Two: $40

Opened in 1989, Mangia Mangia Pasta Café isn't just getting older, it keeps getting better. The restaurant is a continuously changing work in progress. In a city where places go out of business or change hands with alarming regularity, this café's tenure has established it as one of the select dining fixtures of Key West.

The key to its success is its pasta—made fresh on the premises daily. Not only is every order of pasta cooked to order, but so too are the majority of sauces. Featured entrées include Jumbo Shrimp Sautéed in Olive Oil with Fresh Garlic and Shallots, Julienned Prosciutto, Kalamata Olives, Fresh Tomatoes and Imported Romano Cheese. Just prior to serving, the pasta is topped with a mixture of cool, crisp Wild Lettuces dressed with fresh-squeezed Lemon Juice and Extra Virgin Olive Oil. This hot/cool presentation is unique, pungent and refreshing.

Located in a landmark building, the brick patio is home to an exotic collection of palms—some of them endangered. Recently renovated, the restaurant has an updated trattoria feel, complete with Italian tile and mosaic marble borders.

Noted for its wine cellar, Mangia Mangia has been awarded Wine Spectator's Award of Excellence for the past four years.

MANGIA MANGIA'S MENU FOR TWO:

Escargots alla Mangia Mangia

Balsamic Vinaigrette

Mixed Seafood Pasta

Pasta with Fresh Spinach, Tomato, Mushrooms and Chick Peas

Jumbo Shrimp with Rigatoni

Escargots alla Mangia Mangia

Melt the butter in a small skillet over medium heat. Add the olive oil, snails, garlic and shallots. Season with salt and pepper. Cook over medium high heat for about 3 minutes or until the garlic is cooked golden but not brown, and the shallots are translucent.

Add the wine and parsley and reduce the liquid by almost half.

Add the basil at the last moment to keep the fresh flavor and prevent blackening.

Serve 6 escargots over each grilled crouton and spoon enough sauce over each to make a pool on the plate for the crouton to absorb.

Cooking Secret: At Mangia Mangia, we brush diagonally cut, sliced French, Italian or Cuban loaves with an herb- and garlic-infused olive oil and grill them briefly on both sides on a char grill. At home, if not grilling, you may run them under a broiler or toaster oven.

Serves 2
Preparation Time:
 20 Minutes

 1 Tbsp. butter
 1 Tbsp. olive oil
12 snails, rinsed
 1 Tbsp. garlic, chopped
 2 shallots, finely
  chopped
  Salt and pepper to
  taste
¼ cup white wine
 1 tsp. parsley, chopped
 1 bunch fresh basil,
  finely chopped
 2 garlic croutons

☆

Balsamic Vinaigrette

Yield: 3 cups
Preparation Time:
   10 Minutes

   1 cup red wine vinegar
   ½ cup balsamic vinegar
   ¼ cup water
   1½ tsps. dried oregano
   1½ tsps. dried basil
   ½ tsp. black pepper,
      coarsely ground
   1½ Tbsps. fresh garlic,
      finely minced
   1 cup extra virgin olive
      oil
   1 cup pure olive oil

I n a mixing bowl, combine the vinegars, water, spices and garlic. Just before serving add the olive oils. Mix or shake well.

This dressing is delicious served over a salad of mixed romaine and Boston lettuce with sliced red onion and tomato wedges. Add other ingredients as desired, such as fresh basil leaves, peppers, mushrooms, etc.

Cooking Secret: This vinaigrette may be stored in the refrigerator for several days. Use high quality vinegars and olive oils. The little bit of water reduces acidity but retains the fine flavor of the vinegar. Inexpensive vinegars are already too diluted. Look for vinegars in the range of 6% acidity.

This dressing is the only dressing available at Mangia Mangia. Though simple to make, it is delicious, and through the years many customers have requested that we sell the dressing. Well, the mystery is now revealed.

Mixed Seafood Pasta

Heat oil in a 12-inch skillet over medium heat. Add the garlic, seafood and shallot and sear for 1 minute. Add the seasonings and mix into the seafood mixture. Add the white wine and bring to a quick boil. Add the green peas and clam broth and return to a boil. Simmer about 2 minutes until the seafood is cooked through.

Divide over 2 servings of hot pasta served in deep pasta plates or bowls. Garnish with chopped tomato and parmesan cheese.

Cooking Secret: This brothy pasta dish is delicious and full-flavored, yet it has substantially less fat than from many traditional sauces.

Serves 2
Preparation Time:
10 Minutes

2 Tbsps. olive oil
1 Tbsp. fresh garlic, finely chopped
6 jumbo shrimp, peeled, deveined
5 oz. sea scallops
5 oz. fresh fish, cut into large chunks (preferably 2 different varieties and colors, such as mahi mahi and salmon)
2 oz. conch meat, thinly sliced
1 shallot, chopped
$\frac{1}{4}$ tsp. dried thyme, whole
1 Tbsp. fresh basil, chopped
$\frac{1}{4}$ tsp. red pepper flakes
$\frac{1}{4}$ cup dry white wine
$\frac{1}{3}$ cup frozen green peas, thawed
$1\frac{1}{4}$ cups rich clam broth
$\frac{1}{2}$ lb. pasta of your choice, cooked
1 tomato, seeded, chopped for garnish
Parmesan cheese, shaved for garnish

Pasta with Fresh Spinach, Tomato, Mushrooms and Chick Peas

Serves 2
Preparation Time:
   15 Minutes

   ⅓ cup olive oil
   1 cup mushrooms,
      quartered
   2 tsps. garlic
   1 Tbsp. shallot, diced
   ⅓ cup chick peas,
      cooked, rinsed
   2 Tbsps. fresh basil,
      finely chopped
   2 pinches oregano
      Red pepper flakes to
      taste
   1 large tomato, seeded,
      cubed
1½ cups spinach, stems
      removed
      Salt and pepper to
      taste
   ½ lb. pasta of your choice
      Feta cheese for garnish

H eat the olive oil in a 12-inch skillet over medium heat. Add the mushrooms, garlic, shallot and chick peas, and cook until the mushrooms are almost tender and the shallot is translucent. Add the seasonings and continue cooking 30 seconds. Add the tomato and mix into the mushroom mixture. Add the spinach, then cover and steam until it wilts. Stir in the spinach and divide over 2 plates with pasta.

Top each plate with crumbled feta cheese.

Cooking Secret: The colors of this dish are brilliant due to the quick cooking. The bright red of the tomato, the deep green of the spinach and the pure white of the feta cheese combine to make the tri-color so popular in the Italian culture.

★

Jumbo Shrimp with Rigatoni

Heat olive oil in a medium skillet. Add the shrimp, garlic, shallot, prosciutto, salt and peppers. Stir constantly to ensure even cooking of shrimp. When the shrimp appears white and nearly cooked through, about 3 minutes, add the olives and tomato.

Toss the shrimp mixture together enough to heat the tomatoes through, about 1 minute. The dish is finished before the tomatoes appear soft.

Divide the mixture over two plates of well-drained cooked rigatoni. Cover generously with grated Romano cheese.

Serves 2
Preparation Time:
  15 Minutes

¼ cup olive oil
12 jumbo shrimp, peeled, deveined
1 Tbsp. garlic, finely chopped
1 shallot, finely chopped
2 oz. prosciutto, julienned
  Salt and pepper to taste
  Red pepper flakes to taste
8 large kalamata olives
1 large tomato, seeded, cubed
2 servings of rigatoni pasta, cooked
  Fresh Romano cheese, grated for garnish

★

CHEECA LODGE

Mile Marker 82
Islamorada, Florida 33036
(800) 327-2888
(305) 664-4651
Room Rates: $160–$1,500

I n the middle of splendid tropical gardens bursting with majestic palms and vibrant flowers, Cheeca Lodge is situated on a beautiful 27-acre estate with all the comforts of home. Barefoot elegance is their trademark. Just a short stroll from each room is a complete roster of water sports, from snorkeling to parasailing to fishing some of the richest waters in the world. There are two freshwater swimming pools, a saltwater lagoon and meandering ponds to help loll away the hot days. Of course, guests can walk along the palm-lined golden beach and watch the sunset over the crystal-blue waters.

Cheeca Lodge has more than 200 rooms and suites for guests to choose from. All are generously oversized and impeccably decorated. Most have private balconies. The villas have fully-equipped kitchens, 1 or 2 master bedrooms and baths, living rooms and screened-in porches.

Children will enjoy Camp Cheeca, an exciting and well-organized activities program with an emphasis on environmental awareness.

Touted by *Esquire* magazine as "one of the chefs to watch in 1996," Chef Dawn Sieber has created menus that blend traditional Florida Keys recipes with her own style of "new American" cuisine. She is also setting the trend in environmental responsibility in her kitchens by encouraging recycling, removing endangered seafood species like conch from her menus, and featuring more farm-raised seafood.

Roasted Corn and Crab Soup

I n a heavy pot over medium heat, lightly cook vegetables in butter until they become translucent.

While vegetables are sweating, add bay leaf, black pepper, cayenne, leaf thyme, oregano, salt, Old Bay Seasoning and chili powder.

Deglaze with white wine. Reduce. Add heavy cream and half and half. Bring to a boil. Lower heat and simmer until slightly reduced. Mix with a hand blender to purée and then strain.

Garnish bowls of soup with corn kernels, lump crab meat and scallions.

Serves 8
Preparation Time:
30 Minutes

8 ears yellow corn,
   kernels cut from cob
2 fennel bulbs, chopped
2 leeks, diced
1 large onion, chopped
6 celery stalks, chopped
1 jalapeño pepper,
   seeded, chopped
¼ cup butter
1 bay leaf
1 tsp. black pepper
¼ tsp. cayenne
½ tsp. leaf thyme
½ tsp. oregano
1 Tbsp. salt
1 Tbsp. Old Bay
   Seasoning
1 Tbsp. chili powder
2 cups white wine
1 qt. heavy cream
1 qt. half and half
   Corn kernels for
   garnish
   Lump crab meat for
   garnish
   Scallions for garnish

☆

Key Lime and Tamarind Vinaigrette

Yield: About 5 cups
Preparation Time:
5 Minutes
(note soaking time)

8 to 10 fresh tamarind
  pods
1 cup hot water
2 oz. fresh ginger, grated
  Juice from 2 Key limes
½ cup balsamic vinegar
2 cups peanut oil
2 Tbsps. honey
  Salt and pepper to
  taste

S crape and soak tamarind paste and seeds in hot water for 15 minutes. Add ginger, Key lime juice and vinegar. Strain.

Whisk peanut oil in slowly. Add honey, salt and pepper.

☆

White Chocolate Spice Ice Cream with Mango-Vanilla Compote and Tropical Fruit Salsa

For the ice cream: Whisk the egg yolks and sugar together in a double boiler over simmering water until the sugar is dissolved and warm to the touch. Scald the vanilla beans in the half and half. Add the white chocolate and allspice to the half and half and mix with a hand mixer until chocolate is melted. Slowly pour the white chocolate mixture into the egg yolks, stirring constantly. Add the heavy cream and churn until frozen.

For the compote: Boil sugar, water, sour orange juice and Key lime juice and vanilla bean until liquid is clear. Add the mangoes and cook for 15 to 20 more minutes until syrup is slightly thick.

For the salsa: Dice all the fruit. Lightly mix with fruit juices and coconut milk. Ladle over ice cream.

Serves 8
Preparation Time:
  1½ Hours
(note refrigeration time)

Ice Cream:

  12 egg yolks
   1 cup sugar
   2 vanilla beans
   2 cups half and half
   1 cup white chocolate,
     chopped
  ¼ tsp. allspice
   1 qt. heavy cream

Compote:

   1 cup sugar
  ½ cup water
  ¼ cup sour orange juice
     Juice from 1 Key lime
   1 vanilla bean
   2 mangoes

Salsa:

   1 kiwi
  ¼ pineapple
  ½ mango
  ½ papaya
     Juice from 2 passion
     fruits
  ½ cup pineapple juice
   1 Tbsp. coconut milk

☆

HYATT KEY WEST RESORT AND MARINA

601 Front Street
Key West, Florida 33040
(800) 233-1234
(305) 296-9900
Room Rates: $195–$665

Discover a Caribbean-style hideaway in a land where shopping, sightseeing and relaxing days are the law. Where you can pull up a lounge chair and bask poolside on a sun deck, complete with whirlpool and private beach area. The Hyatt Key West Resort and Marina is just steps from the excitement of Duval Street, Old Town's main promenade, Ernest Hemingway's home and studio, the treasure trove of the Wrecker's Museum and the nightly celebration at Mallory Square.

Guests enjoy the private marina, which offers waverunners, sailing, snorkeling, diving and charter fishing, the pool with its landscaped multi-level sun deck and whirlpool and the secluded beach area. Guests have two specialty restaurants to choose from—Nicola Seafood for tempting Caribbean specialties and Nick's Bar and Grill for casual dining and sunset views from the balcony.

Conch Fritters with Honey Mustard Sauce

Place all vegetables in a food processor and grind for 1 minute. Place in a mixing bowl and set aside.

Grind conch meat for 1 minute and add to the bowl. Add the egg, flour, baking powder and spices and gently fold together.

Scoop up with wet hands and mold into small balls, each about 1½ inches in diameter. Place in deep fryer until golden. Serve with sauce on the side.

For the sauce: Place all ingredients in a bowl and mix.

Yield: 15 to 20 pieces
Preparation Time:
  20 Minutes

  2 oz. carrots
  2 oz. green bell peppers
  1 oz. red bell pepper
1½ oz. celery
  1 oz. white onion
  1 tsp. jalapeño, minced
  7 oz. conch meat
  1 egg
1⅓ cups flour
  2 tsps. baking powder
  1 tsp. Tabasco Sauce
  ½ tsp. cayenne pepper
    Oil for deep frying

Sauce:

  1 oz. honey
  1 oz. Dijon mustard
  ½ oz. lime juice
  2 oz. mayonnaise

Conch Chowder

Serves 8
Preparation Time:
 1½ Hours

 ½ lb. conch meat
 1 oz. butter
 2 oz. celery, diced
1½ oz. carrots, diced
 1 oz. green bell pepper,
   diced
 1 oz. red bell pepper,
   diced
1½ oz. white onion, diced
 4 oz. potato, peeled,
   diced
 ½ tsp. jalapeño, minced
 ½ pint clam juice
 ½ pint tomato juice
 ½ tsp. oregano, chopped
 ½ tsp. thyme, chopped
 ½ tsp. garlic, chopped
 ½ tsp. Tabasco Sauce

Grind conch meat in a food processor for 1 minute.
Heat pan and add butter. Sauté all vegetables for 5 minutes. Add juices, herbs and spices. Add conch and simmer for 1 hour.

Taste, adjust seasoning and serve.

Macadamia-Crusted Yellowtail with Mango-Papaya Salsa

Grind nuts and bread crumbs for 30 seconds in a food processor. Place in a bowl.

Dredge fish filets in flour, then the egg and finally in the bread crumb mixture. Salt and pepper to taste. Sauté in oil until golden.

Place Mango Papaya Salsa on plate and top with fish. Garnish with lemon and fresh mint.

For the salsa: Place all the salsa ingredients in a bowl. Let sit and chill for 2 hours.

Serves 4
Preparation Time:
  20 Minutes
(note refrigeration time)

- 3 oz. macadamia nuts
- 2 oz. bread crumbs
- 4 yellowtail filets, bones removed, 5-oz. each
- 2 oz. seasoned flour
- 1 egg, beaten
  Salt and pepper to taste
  Oil
  Lemon wedges for garnish
  Fresh mint sprigs for garnish

Mango Papaya Salsa:

- 3 oz. papaya, diced
- 3 oz. mango, diced
- 1 oz. red bell pepper, diced
- 1 oz. green bell pepper, diced
- 1 tsp. jalapeño, minced
- 1 oz. red onion, diced
- 1 tsp. cilantro, diced
  Juice from 1 lemon
- 3 oz. papaya nectar or other fruit juice

★

MARQUESA HOTEL

600 Fleming Street
Key West, Florida 33040
(800) 869-4631
(305) 292-1919
Room Rates: $135–$325

I magine the convenience of a full service hotel with the intimacy of an inn—the very definition of the Marquesa Hotel. Enter the lobby and you immediately see and feel the qualities that set the Marquesa apart: fresh flowers, antiques, the brilliant lights of Key West flooding in through tall windows. The concierge greets guests and shows them the hotel, answers any questions regarding the island's attractions—and does it all with a sincere smile. Listed on the National Register of Historic Places, the buildings are beautifully restored examples of classic Key West architecture. Guests can lounge by the pool surrounded by palm trees.

Each of the 27 rooms and suites is rich in fabrics and furniture—an elegant mix of traditional and tropical. The bathrooms are highlighted with marble.

Café Marquesa is noted for its unique array of international flavors and wonderful service.

Granola

Place the oats, almonds and sunflower seeds in a large bowl.

Combine the oil, sweeteners, vanilla, almond extract, cinnamon and salt. Heat this mixture in a saucepan until it becomes watery. Pour over the oat mixture and mix well.

Pour the mixture on a large baking pan or cookie sheet.

Bake in the middle of a 325° oven for about 30 minutes, or until the granola turns golden, stirring every 5 minutes so the mixture toasts uniformly.

Transfer to a large bowl or cool baking pan and toss occasionally until the granola is thoroughly cool and dry.

Add the dried fruit and toss to mix.

Store in a tightly covered container.

Yield: 1 lb.
Preparation Time:
  20 Minutes
Preheat oven to 325°

12 cups old fashioned
   rolled oats
 7 cups almonds, coarsely
   chopped
 9 cups sunflower seeds
1½ cups safflower oil or
   soy oil
1½ cups honey
1½ cups maple syrup
 3 Tbsps. vanilla
1½ tsps. almond extract
1½ Tbsps. cinnamon
   Salt to taste
 3 cups or more of any of
   these fruits: raisins,
   currants, dried
   apricots, figs or prunes,
   dates (cut into small
   pieces)

Pan-Seared Snapper Fingerlings with Mushroom and Leek Ragout

Serves 6
Preparation Time:
  30 Minutes

- 4 oz. oyster mushrooms, stems discarded, sliced
- 4 oz. shiitake mushrooms, stems discarded, sliced
- 4 oz. leeks, sliced ⅛-inch thick
- 4 Tbsps. butter
- 4 Tbsps. fish stock
- 6 Tbsps. heavy cream
  Thyme to taste
  Salt and white pepper to taste
- 12 snapper filets, cut into1 oz. portions
  Flour for dredging
- ½ cup vegetable oil
- 2 oz. tomato concassé
- 1 leek, julienned, deep fried for garnish (optional)

I n a medium sauté pan, over medium-high heat, sauté mushrooms and leeks in butter for 10 minutes, tossing frequently. Deglaze pan with fish stock and simmer 3 to 4 minutes. Add heavy cream and simmer for 5 minutes or until slightly thickened. Season with thyme, salt and pepper.

Season snapper with salt and white pepper. Dredge snapper in flour and shake off excess. In a large sauté pan over high heat, add oil and heat until it begins to smoke. Sauté snapper until golden, turn fish, lower heat and cook until fish is just done, 1 to 2 minutes.

To serve: Mound mushroom ragout in center of plate, allowing cream to cover a small portion of plate. Lay fish on ragout, put tomato concassé around and top fish with frizzled leeks.

Grouper with Avocado-Lime Sauce, Black Bean & Corn Relish and Pineapple Risotto

For the grouper: Brush with oil and season. Grill to desired doneness.

For the sauce: Place all ingredients in blender and purée. Adjust seasoning. If consistency is too thick, thin with milk.

For the risotto: Sauté onion, garlic and rice in olive oil. When rice is toasted, add liquids in small increments while stirring often. When rice is firm but creamy, finish with Asiago cheese, salt, white pepper and fresh pineapple.

To serve: Place a generous portion of the avocado-lime sauce on the grouper, which sits on top of the risotto in the center of the plate. Place the bean and corn relish around the plate with the vegetable of your choice.

Black Bean and Corn Relish:

1 cup black beans, cooked
1 ear corn, grilled, cut off the cob
1 red onion, diced fine
1 red bell pepper, diced fine
  Cilantro, chopped to taste
  Salt and white pepper to taste
  Olive oil to coat

For the relish: Mix all ingredients and chill for 2 hours.

Serves 4
Preparation Time:
  1 Hour
(note refrigeration time)

4 grouper filets, 8-oz.
  each
  Oil
  Salt and white pepper

Sauce:

1 ripe avocado
½ red onion
  Juice from 2 limes
  White pepper, salt and
  cumin to taste

Pineapple Risotto:

½ onion, diced
½ Tbsp. garlic
1 cup Arborio rice
1 Tbsp. olive oil
½ cup white wine
1 cup pineapple juice
  Asiago cheese, grated
  to taste
  Salt and white pepper
  to taste
1 pineapple, diced to
  taste

★

MARRIOTT'S CASA MARINA RESORT

1500 Reynolds Street
Key West, Florida 33040
(800) 228-9290
(305) 296-3535
Room Rates: $187–$795

The oldest and largest resort in all the Keys, Marriott's Casa Marina Resort captures the Old Floridian charisma of Key West. It is easy to imagine why Hemingway was so inspired to write and fish by the Key.

Edging up to the resort is Marriott's Kokomo Beach, the largest private beach.

With its white gingerbread trimming and casual island decor, this resort has everything: tennis, wind surfing, fishing, sunset cruises, two oceanside pools and great restaurants.

Crab Cakes with Banana Raisin Chutney

Pit, peel and chop avocado and place in a bowl. Squeeze juice from half the lemon over the avocado to prevent discoloration. Slice remaining lemon half into wedges and reserve for garnish.

Lightly beat the egg in a separate bowl. Stir in the mayonnaise, mustard, chives, dill, cilantro and ½ cup bread crumbs.

Add the crab meat, avocado, peppers and Worcestershire sauce. Stir until just mixed. Season to taste with salt and pepper.

Pat the crab mixture into eight 4-inch cakes. Dredge crab cakes in remaining bread crumbs.

Heat olive oil in a frying pan over medium-high heat until hot but not smoking. Cook the crab cakes, turning once, until golden brown and warmed through, about 4 minutes total. Drain on paper towels.

To serve, place 2 warm crab cakes on each plate and garnish with lemon wedges and chutney.

Serves 4
Preparation Time:
  15 Minutes

1 avocado
1 lemon
1 egg
2 Tbsps. mayonnaise
1 Tbsp. Dijon mustard
1 tsp. chives, chopped
1 tsp. dill, chopped
1 tsp. cilantro, chopped
1 cup fresh bread
  crumbs
1 lb. fresh crab meat
1 red bell pepper, diced
1 green bell pepper,
  diced
  Dash of Worcestershire
  sauce
  Salt and pepper to
  taste
½ cup olive oil
  Chutney (recipe
  follows)

☆

Banana Raisin Chutney

Yield: 1½ cups
Preparation Time:
  30 Minutes

- 1 large onion, finely diced
- 2 Tbsps. peanut oil
- 1 cup white vinegar
- 1 cup fresh orange juice
- 1 lb. ripe bananas, sliced ¼-inch thick
- 1 Tbsp. fresh ginger, grated
- 1 cup raisins
- 1 cup dark brown sugar
- 1 Tbsp. jalapeño pepper, chopped
  Salt, black pepper and allspice to taste

Sweat the onion in a sauté pan with oil over medium heat. Add the vinegar and orange juice and simmer for 10 minutes. Add the remaining ingredients and return to a simmer. Allow to cool to room temperature.

Warm Chicken and Spinach Salad with Raspberry Vinegar

Heat olive oil in a sauté pan. Add the chicken, garlic, shallot, carrots, mushrooms and pine nuts all at once. Sauté quickly over medium heat.

Deglaze with raspberry vinegar and quickly pour over spinach. Toss together in a bowl.

Serve at once on a heated serving dish.

Serves 4
Preparation Time:
  20 Minutes

  3 Tbsps. olive oil
  2 chicken breasts,
    skinned, julienned
  1 clove garlic, chopped
  1 shallot, chopped
  2 fresh carrots, julienned
 16 large button
    mushrooms, sliced
  4 Tbsps. pine nuts
 ½ cup raspberry vinegar
  1 lb. fresh spinach
    leaves, washed, stems
    removed
    Salt and pepper to
    taste

WHISPERS BED AND BREAKFAST

409 William Street
Key West, Florida 33040
(800) 856-SHHH
(305) 294-5969
Room Rates: $75–$175

T he house, listed on the National Register of Historic Places, sits on a sleepy, shaded street within view of the Gulf harbor, and is surrounded by a thirty-block historic district of distinctive 19th century buildings.

Today, ceiling fans whirl above rooms filled with antique furnishings, and congenial guests enjoy the cool porches and lush gardens at one of the island's most unique inns. A full membership at a nearby spa resort is included in your room rate, offering the use of a sauna, steam room, free weights, exercise equipment, pool and private beach.

A full and varied gourmet breakfast, with selections such as lemon dill omelets, honey-maple ham and hot croissants topped with freshly sliced strawberries, is served daily throughout the year, and can be enjoyed either in the dining area or in the tropical gardens.

Eggs Florentine

Mix first 5 ingredients together and keep warm.
In a blender, beat eggs together.
Put butter in omelet pan. Add 1 serving of egg and cook until bottom is set and egg moves freely, then turn egg. Turn off heat as pan is hot enough to finish cooking the egg. Put spinach mixture in center and fold the edges the of egg over.

Serves 6
Preparation Time:
 20 Minutes

20 oz. spinach, cooked
 1 can cheddar cheese
   soup
 2 tsps. mustard
 2 dashes Worcestershire
   sauce
 1 onion, diced, browned
13 eggs
   Butter

☆

Snow Pea and Carrot Omelet

Serves 2
Preparation Time:
  20 Minutes

  1 **carrot**
    Butter
    Rosemary to taste
  2 **Tbsps. scallions**
 12 **snow peas**
    Garlic powder to taste
  4 **eggs, beaten**

U sing a peeler, peel 12 strips from the carrot.
    Melt butter in omelet pan. Add rosemary, scallions, snowpeas and carrot strips. Cook a few seconds. Sprinkle with garlic powder. Add eggs. When set, turn whole omelet over and let the other side set, then fold the omelet and serve.

☆

Sour Cream Waffles with Raspberry, Strawberry and Cranberry Sauce

I n a bowl, beat eggs with a whisk until light. Whisk in sour cream. Sift in dry ingredients. Whisk until mixed. Add butter, mixing thoroughly. Spray nonstick spray on griddle once before cooking.

Use 1 cup of mix for a 4-section waffle iron. Cook according to waffle iron directions.

Garnish with sauce.

For the sauce: Put strawberries, 1½ cups orange juice and sugar in a pan over low heat until warm. Add ½ cup more orange juice that has been mixed with cornstarch. Cook until mixture is thickened. Turn off the heat and add raspberries and cranberries. Fold in, trying to keep berries whole. Spoon mixture over sour cream waffles.

Serves 12
Preparation Time:
  30 Minutes

  6 **eggs**
  3 **cups sour cream**
  3 **cups flour**
  9 **Tbsps. sugar**
1½ **tsps. baking soda**
 15 **Tbsps. butter, melted**

Sauce:

  1 **bag frozen**
    strawberries
  2 **cups orange juice**
    Sugar to taste
  3 **Tbsps. cornstarch**
  1 **carton frozen**
    raspberries
 ½ **cup frozen cranberries**

AMICI

ITALIAN CUISINE
288 South County Road
Palm Beach, Florida 33480
(561)832-0201
Lunch Monday–Saturday 11:30AM–3PM
Dinner Monday–Thursday 5:30PM–10:30PM
Dinner Friday & Saturday 5:30PM–11PM
Dinner Sunday 5:30 PM–10:30PM
Average Dinner for Two: $95

Step through the doors into the charming European ambiance of Amici, Palm Beach's hottest "in" place to see and be seen. Arches and stucco walls enhance contemporary murals and a daring touch reminiscent of Christo—painted islands suspended from the lamp fixtures. Lively fresh sunflowers are on every table, along with bottles of seasoned olive oil.

Amici quickly gained fame by serving award-winning innovative daily specials, homemade pastas and sauces and a selection of fresh fish daily. Among the celebrated pastas are Pappardelle Amici, a blend of the wide noodles with vine-ripened fresh tomato, basil and mozzarella, and Tagliolini with Shrimp, Asparagus and Fresh Garlic in a Sun-Dried Tomato Sauce. Dinner entrées offer a Tuscan-Style Chicken in Lemon Sage Sauce and Herb-Crusted Veal Chop on a bed of Sautéed Spinach and Cherry Tomatoes in Marsala au Jus. Freshly baked pizzas from the wood-burning oven add a delightful variety to the menu.

AMICI'S MENU FOR TWO:

Risotto with Asparagus and Gorgonzola

Asparagus Piemontesi

Filet Mignon Toscano

Risotto with Asparagus and Gorgonzola

S auté the onion in a sauté pan with olive oil until brown. Add the rice and stir until evenly coated. Add half of the broth, stirring constantly. While maintaining a slow boil, add the asparagus and the rest of the chicken broth, a little at a time, stirring constantly. When all the broth has been absorbed, stir in the cheeses.

The rice is done when it is tender but firm to the bite.

Serves 2
Preparation Time:
 30 Minutes

½ onion, chopped fine
2 Tbsps. extra virgin
  olive oil
1 cup dry Arborio rice
3 cups chicken broth or
  stock
⅓ lb. asparagus, cut thin
⅓ lb. Gorgonzola
  Grated Parmesan to
  taste

Asparagus Piemontesi

Serves 2
Preparation Time:
  15 Minutes

12 jumbo asparagus
 2 Tbsps. ricotta cheese,
    at room temperature
 2 Tbsps. butter
 2 fresh sage sprigs
¼ cup Parmesan cheese,
    shaved
    Fresh white truffles,
    sliced (optional)

lace asparagus in boiling water for 2 minutes, then arrange on 2 serving plates. Place ricotta just below tips of asparagus.

In a sauté pan, heat the butter and sage until browned and pour over the asparagus.

Sprinkle Parmesan cheese and truffles over the entire plate.

★

Filet Mignon Toscano

Sauté the porcini mushrooms in a sauté pan in 1 Tbsp. olive oil until they are golden brown.

Slice the filet mignon into 4 pieces. Place each piece in between two pieces of plastic wrap and pound with a meat tenderizer or bottom of a pan until it is less than ¼-inch thick. These pieces should cover the entire bottom of a dinner plate.

Spread the porcini mushrooms over the meat and place in a 400° oven for about 2 minutes, or until desired doneness is achieved. Carefully remove hot plate from oven.

Top with Parmesan cheese, arugula, salt, pepper and the remaining extra virgin olive oil.

Serves 2
Preparation Time:
30 Minutes
Preheat oven to 400°

¼ **lb. porcini mushrooms,**
   sliced
3 **Tbsps. extra virgin**
   olive oil
2 **filet mignon steaks,**
   8 oz. each
¼ **cup Parmesan cheese,**
   shaved
¼ **cup arugula, julienned**
   Salt and pepper to
   taste

★

THE BISTRO

CONTINENTAL CUISINE
2611 Ponce de Leon Boulevard
Coral Gables, Florida 33134
(305) 442-9671
Lunch Tuesday–Friday 11:30AM–2PM
Dinner Tuesday–Saturday 6PM–11PM
Average Dinner For Two: $65

T his intimate restaurant has been a star in Florida's restaurant landscape since 1977. Executive Chef Hans Klein has kept an eye on trends, tastes and techniques, while developing and maintaining a menu that is a mixture of old favorites and new culinary inspirations. His talent has earned him the respect and admiration of his peers.

Menu favorites for more than 20 years that bring the locals back time and time again are the Chicken Curry Bombay with Fried Bananas and Pineapples and the New Zealand Rack of Lamb with Dijon Mustard, Garlic-Herb Crust and Mint Sauce. Other favorites are Crispy Roasted Duck with a Tamarind-Chipotle Glaze served with Mashed Plantains and the Mushroom Ravioli with Fresh Parmesan and Herbs.

THE BISTRO'S MENU FOR FOUR:

Vegetable Ratatouille

Shrimp and Corn Chowder with Yucca

Grouper à la Chef René

Vegetable Ratatouille

Heat olive oil in a large skillet and sauté the onion over medium heat, cooking until translucent. Stir in the eggplant, bell peppers, tomatoes, corn and okra. Add the garlic, thyme, oregano, salt and pepper and cook over low heat for 15 minutes. Add the zucchini and cook for 5 more minutes. Adjust the seasonings to taste. Add the vinegar and sprinkle with basil before serving.

Serves 4 to 8
Preparation Time:
  30 Minutes

½ cup olive oil
1 lb. onion, cut into
  1-inch cubes
1 lb. eggplant, trimmed,
  cut into 1-inch cubes
½ lb. red bell peppers,
  cored, seeded, cut into
  1-inch cubes
½ lb. yellow bell peppers,
  cored, seeded, cut into
  1-inch cubes
1 lb. ripe tomatoes,
  trimmed, seeded, cut
  into 1-inch cubes
1 fresh ear of corn,
  cooked, cut off cob
4 pieces of okra
2 cloves garlic, minced
1 large fresh thyme sprig
1 large fresh oregano
  sprig
1 tsp. salt
½ tsp. white pepper
½ lb. zucchini, trimmed,
  cut into 1-inch cubes
2 Tbsps. sherry wine
  vinegar
4 to 6 fresh basil leaves,
  chopped

★

Shrimp and Corn Chowder with Yucca

Serves 6
Preparation Time:
  45 Minutes

  1 qt. milk
  1 qt. clam juice, boiled
  2 cups water
  2 Tbsps. paprika
  2 lbs. medium shrimp,
    shelled, deveined, tails
    removed, cut in half
    lengthwise, reserving
    the shells
  4 bacon slices, cut into
    bite-sized pieces
  1 yellow onion, diced
    small
  2 celery stalks, diced
    small
  1 Tbsp. garlic, minced
  1 cup corn kernels
  1 cup yucca, peeled,
    diced
    Salt and black pepper
    to taste

I n a large stock pot, combine the milk, clam juice, water, paprika and shrimp shells. Bring to a boil over medium-high heat, reduce the heat to low and simmer for 20 minutes. Strain, discard the shells and set aside the liquid.

In the same stock pot, cook the bacon over medium-high heat until crisp, about 7 minutes, then remove and drain on paper towels or brown paper bags.

Drain all but about 2 Tbsps. of bacon fat from the pot. Add the onion and celery and cook, stirring frequently, until the onion is translucent, about 5 to 7 minutes. Add the garlic and cook, stirring frequently, for 1 minute.

Add the corn, yucca and reserved liquid and bring to a boil. Reduce the heat to low and simmer for 30 minutes or until the yucca is tender but not mushy. During the last 4 minutes of simmering, add the shrimp and cooked bacon to the pot. Season with salt and pepper and serve.

☆

Grouper à la Chef René

or the batter: In a mixing bowl beat the eggs. Add the beer, salt and pepper. Mix in the flour, blending until smooth. Refrigerate for 30 minutes.

For the grouper: Dust the filets in flour. Dip completely in the batter. Shake off excess batter. Brown lightly in a good oil. Bake in the oven until crispy.

For the sauce: Melt the butter in a saucepan. Add the tomatoes, onion, capers and parsley. Simmer for 5 minutes, leaving the onions firm. Add the wine and seasonings. Keep warm.

To serve, place filets on a serving platter and drizzle with sauce. Sprinkle with almonds and parsley and garnish with lemon wedges.

Serves 6
Preparation Time:
  45 Minutes
(note refrigeration time)
Preheat oven to 400°

Batter:

  4 eggs
  1 cup beer
    Salt and pepper to
    taste
  2 cups flour

Grouper:

  2½ to 3 lbs. grouper filets
  ½ cup flour
  ½ cup oil

Sauce:

  1 cup butter
  1 cup tomatoes, peeled,
    diced
  ½ cup onion, chopped
  ⅓ cup capers
  ⅛ cup parsley, chopped
  1 cup white wine
    Salt and pepper to
    taste
    Almonds, sliced,
    toasted for garnish
    Parsley, chopped for
    garnish
    Lemon wedges for
    garnish

☆

CAFÉ SEVILLE

SPANISH CUISINE
2768 East Oakland Boulevard
Fort Lauderdale, Florida 33306
(954) 565-1148
Lunch Tuesday–Friday 11:30AM–2PM
Dinner Tuesday–Saturday 5:30PM–10PM
Dinner Sunday 5:30PM–9:30PM
Average Dinner for Two: $60

For the taste and feel of traditional Spain, Café Seville offers dishes that range across regions, from gazpacho to roasted pork flavored by a marinade of lemon, garlic, oregano and white wine, to the famous paella. Some things are far more impressive than others, but overall Café Seville executes its large menu and lengthy list of daily specials with skill and style.

A charming dining room with Moorish carvings, framed posters and pottery adorning the adobe-peach walls evokes images of the Old World. The service is professional and efficient and the wine list offers an array of fine vintages and vineyards from $13 to $200.

CAFÉ SEVILLE'S MENU FOR SIX:

Garlic Shrimp

Gazpacho Andaluz

Catalan Custard

Garlic Shrimp

I n a sauté pan or skillet over medium-high heat, heat the olive oil and sauté the shrimp for 2 minutes.

Add the remaining ingredients. Sauté for 2 minutes more or until the shrimp are just evenly pink and slightly curled.

Serve immediately.

Serves 6
Preparation Time:
10 Minutes

2 Tbsps. olive oil
1 lb. medium shrimp, shelled
4 cloves garlic, minced
Pinch of dried red pepper flakes
2 tsps. beef or veal broth
2 tsps. fresh lemon juice
2 tsps. dry sherry
2 tsps. fresh parsley, minced
Salt and white pepper to taste

Gazpacho Andaluz

Serves 6
Preparation Time:
   30 Minutes
(note refrigeration time)

1½ lbs. ripe tomatoes,
   chopped
1 medium green bell
   pepper, cored, seeded,
   chopped
1 small onion, chopped
1 small cucumber,
   peeled, chopped
½ cup olive oil
2 stale French bread
   rolls, broken into
   pieces
1 cup tomato juice
¼ cup red wine vinegar
¼ tsp. dried thyme
1 clove garlic, chopped
1 tsp. salt
   White pepper to taste
2 Tbsps. each: cucumber,
   green pepper, onion,
   diced for garnish
   Croutons for garnish

n a large, non-aluminum bowl, place all the ingredients except the salt, pepper and garnishes. Add water to cover and refrigerate overnight.

In a blender or food processor, purée the chilled mixture. Strain, add salt and pepper and chill.

Garnish with vegetables and croutons.

Catalan Custard

I n a small bowl, beat the eggs with the flour until smooth.

In a saucepan over medium heat, bring the milk just to a boil with the sugar, cinnamon stick, lemon zest and vanilla extract.

Remove the cinnamon stick with a slotted spoon. Slowly add the egg-flour mixture, stirring constantly until the custard is thick and smooth. Allow to just reach the boiling point and then immediately remove it from the heat.

Strain through a fine sieve, pouring into 6 individual clay or oven-proof dishes, and refrigerate until well chilled.

To serve, preheat the broiler. Sprinkle brown sugar evenly over the top of each custard and dust with cinnamon. Place under the broiler until the sugar caramelizes, about 2 to 3 minutes.

Let cool before serving.

Serves 6
Preparation Time:
 25 Minutes
(note refrigeration time)

 4 **whole eggs**
 ½ **cup unbleached, all-**
    purpose flour
 4 **cups milk**
 ⅔ **cup granulated sugar**
 1 **cinnamon stick**
    Zest from ½ lemon
 ¼ **tsp. vanilla extract**
 ⅓ **cup light brown sugar**
    Ground cinnamon to
    taste

☆

CALIFORNIA CAFÉ BAR AND GRILL

CALIFORNIA AND MEDITERRANEAN CUISINE
2301 Southeast 17th Street Causeway
Fort Lauderdale, Florida 33316
(954) 728-3500
Web Site: www.calcafe.com/lauderdale
Average Dinner for Two: $75

California Café Bar and Grill emphasizes creative preparation and presentation of California and Mediterranean fusion cuisine with Caribbean and Pacific Rim accents. Fresh seafood, grilled and rotisserie-roasted meats, gourmet pastas, specialty salads and exotic first courses are the foundation of the menu. Seasonal items from local and regional growers and producers, as well as custom-grown produce from California and in-season seafood from local waters are incorporated.

The design and decor are keyed to the restaurant's prime location on the intra-coastal waterway and the famous Pier 66 Marina. Clean and clear California and Caribbean colors and whimsical designs give the restaurant a bright and lively atmosphere.

Some of the savory dishes not to miss are the Macadamia Nut-Crusted Snapper in Vodka Grapefruit Sauce, Spicy Barbecued Baby Back Ribs served with Peanut Slaw and the wood rotisserie Rosemary Chicken, which is paired with a delightful Apple Chutney and served with Buttermilk-Chive Mashed Potatoes.

CALIFORNIA CAFÉ BAR AND GRILL'S MENU FOR FOUR:

Rock Lobster in Tamarind Thai Coconut Broth

Dolphin with Black Bean Salsa, Plantains and Mango Scotch Bonnet BBQ Sauce

White Chocolate Mousse with Oreo Cookie Crust

Rock Lobster in Tamarind Thai Coconut Broth

lace lobster stock, garlic, lemon grass, coconut milk, tamarind and heavy cream in a pot over low heat and reduce by half.

In a heavy-bottomed pot, heat the olive oil until it is very hot. Add the lobster and sauté until it is well seared.

Add the shallots and garlic. Deglaze with brandy and add the lobster cream reduction.

Bring the mixture to a boil and add the curry paste. Reduce to a light simmer and cook until the lobster is tender.

Add the peas and tomatoes and season to taste with salt, pepper and mirin.

To serve, pour into a large serving bowl and garnish with green onion and lemon zest.

Serves 4
Preparation Time:
 25 Minutes

 4　cups lobster stock
 ½ tsp. garlic, crushed
 2　tsps. lemon grass, crushed
 2　cups coconut milk
 1　Tbsp. tamarind
 1　cup heavy cream
 1　Tbsp. olive oil
 2　lobster tails, diced
 4　shallots, minced
 4　cloves garlic, thinly sliced
 ¼ cup brandy
 ½ Tbsp. green curry paste
 ¼ cup green peas
 ¼ cup tomatoes, diced
 　Salt and pepper to taste
 　Mirin to taste
 　Green onion, sliced for garnish
 　Lemon zest for garnish

Dolphin with Black Bean Salsa, Plantains and Mango Scotch Bonnet BBQ Sauce

Serves 4
Preparation Time:
  1 Hour

  6 red bell peppers
  2 cups cider vinegar
  2 cups brown sugar
  6 ripe mangoes, peeled,
      seeded
  1 Scotch bonnet chile,
      seeded
  1 tsp. ground cloves
  1 onion, peeled,
      chopped
      Salt and pepper to
      taste
  4 dolphin or mahi mahi
      filets
  2 plantains, sliced
      lengthwise
      Salt and pepper to
      taste

Black Bean Salsa:

  4 cups black beans,
      cooked
  1 red pepper, diced
  1 green pepper, diced
  1 red onion, diced
  1 jalapeño pepper, diced
  1 bunch cilantro,
      chopped
  1 Tbsp. garlic, minced
  4 Tbsps. lime juice
  2 Tbsps. olive oil
  1 Tbsp. coriander
  1 Tbsp. cumin
      Salt and pepper

Prepare a charcoal fire and soak a handful of mesquite wood chips in water. When the coals are ready, put the wet wood chips over the coals and place the red peppers on the grill's grate on the highest setting. Put the lid down and smoke the peppers for about 30 minutes. When the peppers are cool, peel and seed them.

In a large saucepan, place the red peppers, vinegar, sugar, mangoes, Scotch bonnet chile, cloves and onion. Cook over medium heat for about 45 minutes, stirring occasionally.

Remove from heat and pour into a blender and purée until smooth. Strain and keep warm. Season with salt and pepper to taste.

Grill dolphin filets along with the plantains for about 4 minutes per side.

To serve, place a filet over a pool of sauce and top with salsa and plantain slices.

For the salsa: Mix all the ingredients together in a bowl and blend well.

White Chocolate Mousse with Oreo Cookie Crust

For the crust: Butter the bottom and sides of cylindrical molds 3 inches high.

Process the cookie crumbs and melted butter in a food processor. Press into the bottom of the molds.

Bring ¾ cup whipping cream to a boil and add the dark chocolate, whisking until melted. Pour over the cookie crumbs and then chill the molds.

For the filling, combine 1 cup of the whipping cream with the white chocolate and melt in a double boiler.

Sprinkle gelatin into the water to dissolve. Set aside.

Whip the remaining 2 cups whipping cream and add the dissolved gelatin. Fold into the melted chocolate. Pour into molds and chill overnight.

To serve, unmold the mousses. Top with shaved white chocolate. On a plate, place the mousse in the center. Arrange raspberries, blackberries and passion fruit slices around the mousse. Garnish with Oreo cookies and grated dark chocolate.

Serves 4
Preparation Time:
  45 Minutes
(note refrigeration time)

  ¼ cup sweet butter, melted
1½ cups Oreo cookie crumbs
3¾ cups whipping cream
  8 oz. dark chocolate, chopped
  1 lb. white chocolate
  1 Tbsp. gelatin
  ¼ cup water
    White chocolate, shaved, for garnish
    Raspberries for garnish
    Blackberries for garnish
    Passion fruit, sliced for garnish
    Oreo cookies for garnish
    Dark chocolate, grated for garnish

DAMIANO'S AT THE TARRIMORE HOUSE

TRANSCONTINENTAL AND FLORASIAN CUISINE
52 North Swinton
Delray Beach, Florida 33447
(407) 272-4706
Dinner Tuesday–Sunday 6PM–10PM
Average Dinner For Two: $80

Anthony and Lisa Damiano have made loyal fans throughout the Sunshine State with their trademark "Florasian" cuisine, uniting the bounty of Florida with the clean, elegant tastes of Asia. Critics are at no loss for words to describe the spectacular fare at this four-star restaurant housed in an exquisite landmark home in the heart of Delray Beach's Pineapple District. The menu offers a cross-cultural marriage of flavors encompassing dishes that bridge the European continent.

The Damianos have been delighting diners since their New York days, when Tony was executive chef and Lisa took over the dessert kitchen at the famous Russian Tea Room. Together, they have established an extensive "fat-free" menu, using techniques for deepening flavors while drastically cutting fat and calories.

Some of the globe-trotting recipes are Tea-Smoked Duck and Asian Vegetable Ravioli, Yukon Gold Potatoes, Florasian Lacquered Duck à la Chiles, Ostrich Kulebiaka and Key Lime Mousse Tart.

DAMIANO'S AT THE TARRIMORE HOUSE'S MENU FOR FOUR:

Mushrooms à la Russe

Low-Fat Southwestern Tacoless Summer Salad

Grilled Soft-Shell Crabs with Mango, Jicama and Tomatillo Salsa

Sesame-Crusted Angelic Drunken Peach Trifle

Mushrooms à la Russe

Boil the mushrooms in salted water for 5 to 10 minutes. Drain and chop fine.

Mix with the remaining ingredients. Season to taste.

Serve on the bread slices.

Serves 4
Preparation Time:
  20 Minutes

½ lb. mushrooms
  Salt
⅓ cup onion, chopped
  fine
2 Tbsps. vegetable oil
1 Tbsp. fresh dill,
  chopped fine
2 tsps. white wine
  vinegar
1 tsp. Dijon mustard
  Salt and pepper to
  taste
1 loaf French or dark rye
  bread, cut into ½-inch
  slices, buttered,
  toasted

☆

Low-Fat Southwestern Tacoless Summer Salad

Serves 4 to 6
Preparation Time:
  25 Minutes

  5 mists of olive oil spray
  1 Vidalia onion, diced
  4 cloves garlic, chopped
  1 lb. lean ground beef
  1 tomato, diced
3½ tsps. Southwestern
    spices: cayenne, cumin,
    chili powder, paprika
    and oregano
    Salt and pepper to
    taste
  ¼ tsp. Scotch bonnet or
    habañero chile, diced
  1 head Romaine lettuce
  1 head Red leaf lettuce
  1 bunch fresh spinach
  6 oz. fat-free cheddar
    cheese, grated
  4 Tbsps. fat-free sour
    cream
  6 scallions, diced

ist a sauté pan over medium heat with the olive oil spray. Add the onion and garlic and cook until translucent.

Add the ground beef and brown while stirring constantly. Add the fresh tomato and then sprinkle in the spices and the hot chile. Cook for another minute, then set aside.

Chop the lettuces and place in serving bowls. Sprinkle the meat over the lettuce and top with cheddar cheese, sour cream and scallions.

☆

Grilled Soft-Shell Crabs with Mango, Jicama and Tomatillo Salsa

I n a medium bowl, combine the tomatillos, tomatoes, half of the onion, ¼ cup of the cilantro, chile flakes, salt and pepper. Toss and set aside for 5 minutes, then add 2 Tbsps. of the lime juice and set aside.

In a medium bowl, combine the mango, jicama, cucumber, the remaining onion and cilantro, and then drizzle in ¼ cup of the olive oil. Add the lime juices and mix well. Season with salt and pepper. Set aside.

Preheat the grill to medium heat and spray on non-stick oil or brush the grill with olive oil. Brush the crabs with the oil and garlic, place on the hot grill and cook until they are golden brown on both sides.

Serve soft-shell crabs on a bed of mango, cucumber and jicama salad, topped with the salsa.

Serves 6
Preparation Time:
  45 Minutes

½ cup tomatillos, husked, diced
¾ cup tomatoes, diced
1 medium Vidalia onion, peeled, finely chopped
½ cup cilantro, chopped
2 tsps. ancho chile flakes
  Salt and pepper to taste
4 Tbsps. lime juice
¾ cup mango, peeled, diced
1½ cups jicama, peeled, julienned
1 cup cucumber, seedless
½ cup extra virgin olive oil
2 Tbsps. Key lime juice
1 clove garlic, peeled, minced
6 soft-shell crabs

Sesame-Crusted Angelic Drunken Peach Trifle

Serves 8
Preparation Time:
1 Hour
(note marinating and refrigeration times)
Preheat oven to 325°

  8 Georgia peaches, pitted, sliced
  2 Tbsps. + 1 tsp. Grand Marnier
  2 Tbsps. dark rum
2½ tsps. vanilla extract
    Vegetable spray
  1 cup black and white sesame seeds, roasted for coating
  1 cup cake flour, sifted twice
1⅓ cups powdered sugar
 ¼ tsp. salt
12 large egg whites
1½ tsps. cream of tartar
  1 cup sugar
  2 tsps. orange zest, finely grated
    Pastry cream (recipe follows)

Combine peaches with 2 Tbsps. Grand Marnier, rum and 1½ tsps. vanilla. Marinate at least 1 hour.

Spray springform, Bundt or muffin pan for individual trifles with vegetable spray and sprinkle sesame seeds in pan around the bottom and sides of the mold. Set aside.

Sift the flour, powdered sugar and salt onto waxed paper.

Whip the egg whites until frothy. Then add the cream of tartar and whip faster until soft peaks form.

Add the sugar slowly in a steady stream.

Fold ¼ of the flour mixture into the egg whites, using a rubber spatula. Gently folding, add 1 tsp. vanilla, then add ¼ more of the flour. Add 1 tsp. Grand Marnier and then add the rest of the flour mixture. Fold in the orange zest last.

Pour the batter into the pan of your choice. Bake in the bottom third of the oven until golden and springy to the touch, about 45 to 50 minutes.

Remove from oven and cool on wire rack. Invert and remove pan. Set aside until ready to build. Once cooled, cut cake into 3 layers.

To serve, begin with one of the 3 layers of cake. Place on a decorative platter, and spread one third of the pastry cream, evenly on the cake layer. Spoon the drunken peaches on top of the pastry cream. Repeat with the remaining 2 cake layers, pastry cream and peaches.

★

Pastry Cream

or the cream: In a mixing bowl, beat the egg whites and sugar together and then add flour and mix until well blended.

In a heavy-bottomed saucepan, heat the milk on medium-high until scalding. Add the milk to the flour mixture and stir until well blended. Pour back into the saucepan, and, using a wooden spoon, stir constantly until it begins to thicken. Reduce heat to medium-low and continue cooking and stirring for 3 more minutes.

Remove from heat and stir in liqueur, vanilla and salt. Place plastic wrap directly on top of the pastry cream, with a little corner uncovered, and refrigerate for about 1 hour.

Preparation Time:
30 Minutes
(note refrigeration time)

3 egg whites
5 Tbsps. sugar
2 Tbsps + 2 tsps. all-
   purpose flour
1 cup skim milk
1 tsp. Grand Marnier
1 tsp. vanilla extract
   Pinch of salt

FIFTH AVENUE GRILL

STEAKHOUSE AND TRADITIONAL AMERICAN CUISINE
821 Southeast 5th Avenue
Delray Beach, Florida 33483
(561) 265-0122
Lunch Daily 11:30AM–2:30PM
Dinner Sunday–Saturday 5PM–10PM
Average Dinner for Two: $75

If you are in the mood for a great steak, Fifth Avenue Grill is your destination. Opened in 1989 at a time when Americans were disdaining meat, the Grill (as it is affectionately known by locals) built its reputation as the steakhouse in Palm Beach County. The hum of dinner conversation from other well-fed diners creates a real English-tavern-style atmosphere. The little extras, such as warm French bread, unlimited salad and fresh vegetables to snack on delivered to the table, are what make each diner feel special, whether it is their first time or their hundredth time there.

The menu is overwhelmingly good, hearty comfort food. The specialties of the menu are Grilled Swordfish with Three-Peppercorn Butter, Prime Aged Boneless New York Sirloin, a very fresh Yellowfin Tuna accompanied by Caribbean Salsa and the Prime Roast Rib of Beef with Yorkshire Pudding. The wine list is extensive, featuring select California and French varietals.

FIFTH AVENUE GRILL'S MENU FOR TWO:

Shrimp de Jonge

Belgian Endive Salad with Citrus Vinaigrette

Steak Fromage

Shrimp de Jonge

For the sauce: Melt the butter in a saucepan and sauté the shallots until they are translucent. Add the sherry and reduce by half. Add the cream, salt and pepper and reduce again by half, or to a nice, thick consistency. Add parsley and set aside.

For the topping: Combine all the ingredients in a food processor until well blended. Set aside.

For the shrimp: Sauté the shrimp for 2 minutes on each side in butter. Transfer to an oven-proof dish and top with the bread crumb topping mixture. Heat at 400° for 6 to 8 minutes or until brown. Transfer to platter and top with the sauce and fresh chives.

Serves 2
Preparation Time:
  40 Minutes
Preheat oven to 400°

Sauce:

  ½ Tbsp. butter
  1 Tbsp. shallots
  ¼ cup sherry
  ¾ cup heavy cream
    Salt and white pepper
    to taste
  1 tsp. parsley, chopped

Bread Crumb Topping:

  1 lb. butter, room
    temperature
  ⅓ cup shallots
  5 cloves garlic, chopped
  2 cups bread crumbs
  ½ Tbsp. Worcestershire
    sauce
  1 Tbsp. dry mustard
  ½ tsp. white pepper
  ½ tsp. Dijon mustard

Shrimp:

  10 large shrimp
  ½ Tbsp. butter
  1 Tbsp. fresh chives

★

Belgian Endive Salad with Citrus Vinaigrette

Serves 2
Preparation Time:
  15 Minutes

   3 cups fresh orange juice
  ½ cup fresh lime juice
   3 Tbsps. ginger root,
     minced
1½ Tbsps. Dijon mustard
  ⅓ cup sugar
  ⅓ cup Grand Marnier
   3 cups extra virgin olive
     oil
  ¾ cup red wine vinegar
   2 tsps. salt and freshly
     cracked black pepper
  ½ tsp. red pepper flakes
   5 Belgian endives,
     chopped
   2 cups mixed baby
     greens
   1 tomato, peeled,
     seeded, diced

 or the vinaigrette: Combine the orange juice, lime juice and ginger in a saucepan over medium heat and reduce by half. Set aside.

In a food processor, combine the mustard, sugar and Grand Marnier. Pulse until smooth.

Add the olive oil slowly, alternating with the red wine vinegar. Finish the dressing by slowly adding the citrus mixture, salt, pepper and pepper flakes.

In a salad bowl combine the endive with the baby greens and add dressing to taste. Toss well and garnish with diced tomatoes.

☆

Steak Fromage

I n a sauté pan over medium heat, sauté the shallots in olive oil until translucent. Add the red wine and reduce by half.

Add the brown sauce and cook for 6 to 10 minutes.

Grill the filet to the desired degree at doneness. Top with Boursin cheese and melt under a 400° broiler for 2 minutes.

Place the red wine sauce over the entire plate, with the sautéed mushrooms in each corner and tomatoes in between. Place a filet in the middle of the plate. Garnish with parsley.

Cooking Secret: Brown sauce is known in France as espagnole sauce. Brown sauce is used as a base for dozens of other sauces. It's traditionally made of a rich meat stock, a myriad of browned vegetables, a brown roux, herbs and sometimes tomato paste.

Serves 2
Preparation Time:
  25 Minutes

  1 Tbsp. shallots, chopped
  1 Tbsp. olive oil
  1 cup red wine
  1 cup brown sauce or
    espagnole sauce
  2 filet mignons, 8 oz.
    each
  5 oz. Boursin cheese
  8 mushrooms, stemmed
  1 tomato, peeled,
    seeded, diced
    Fresh parsley, chopped
    for garnish

GRAND CAFE

NEW FLORIDA CUISINE
Grand Bay Hotel
2669 South Bayshore Drive
Coconut Grove, Florida
(888) 80-GRAND
(305) 858-9600
Web Site: www.grandbay.com
Breakfast Daily 7AM–11AM
Lunch Monday–Saturday 11:30AM–3PM
Lunch Buffet Monday–Friday 11:30AM–3PM
Dinner Sunday–Thursday 6PM–11PM, Friday & Saturday 6PM–11:30PM
Brunch Sunday 11:30AM–3PM
Average Dinner for Two: $82

Located in Miami's premier hotel, Grand Cafe stands on its own as a premier restaurant. Seated in a luxurious setting of polished woods, lavish flowers and a live jazz ensemble, diners senses are inundated with the sights, sounds, smells and tastes associated with a out-of-the-ordinary dining experience.

Executive Chef Pascal Oudin is one of the founding chefs of New Florida cuisine. His dishes are firmly rooted in classical French cuisine traditions but with more modern sensibilities. He takes full advantage of Florida's cornucopia of local fresh food. Grand Cafe and Chef Oudin have both received many accolades including "America's Best New Chefs" by Food & Wine Magazine and "Best in Dade County" by South Florida Magazine.

Choosing what to eat is difficult when the menu is loaded with tasty choices: Veal and Sun-Dried Tomato Ravioli, Jumbo Sea Scallops and Portobello Mushroom Gratin, Lobster and Green Asparagus Risotto, She Crab Soup, Steamed and Roasted Vegetable Torte, Star Anise Scented Grilled Mahi Mahi, Tropical Tiramisu and Key Lime and Cheesecake Tatinlette.

Grand Cafe has a superior wine list including over 60 aged rums and tequilas.

GRAND CAFE'S MENU FOR FOUR

Pan-Seared Bahamian Conch Cake with Yucca Stalk and Lemon Grass Sauce

Mango "Tarte Tatin" with Banana Ice Cream and Kumquat Aspic

Pan-Seared Bahamian Conch Cake with Yucca Stalk and Lemon Grass Sauce

For the custard: Peel and clean the shrimp. Then place in a blender with the whole eggs, egg yolk, Old Bay Seasonings, salt and pepper. Blend together to purée. Add the heavy cream and process until blended. Taste and correct seasoning if necessary. Transfer to a bowl and place over ice. Place aside and reserve.

For the sauce: Rinse the snapper bones and drain well.

Slowly melt the sweet butter in a heavy sauce pot over medium heat. Add garlic, shallots, ginger, celery, lemon grass and annatto seed powder, cover and sweat for five minutes. Remove lid and add fish bones. Cover again and sweat five more minutes. Then, remove lid and turn heat to medium-high. Add vermouth and reduce by ½. Add chicken broth and reduce by ½. Add 2 cups heavy cream and coconut milk and cook for ten minutes more and strain off liquid. Discard bones and return sauce to heat. Reduce to desired consistency. Place in a blender and blend to smooth texture. Strain and check seasoning.

For the cake: In a mixing bowl, add the conch meat and cilantro. Fold the mixture into the reserved shrimp custard.

In a small sauté pan over high heat, add olive oil. Place a flan ring in the center. Spoon mixture into the ring making a perfect circle. Removing ring and cook on one side only for two minutes over medium heat. Bake in a 350° oven for 3 to 5 minutes. Remove from oven and turn the conch cake over.

For the garnishes: Combine vanilla powder, salt and cayenne pepper and set aside.

Peel and cut the yucca into thick julienne and fry them in grapeseed oil. Sprinkle with vanilla mix.

To serve: Pour the sauce on the plate and place the conch cake in the center of the plate. Garnish with crisp yucca stalk on top of the cake.

* Annatto is a derivative of achiote seed, commercial annatto paste and powder is used to color butter, margarine, cheese and smoked fish.

Serves 4
Preparation Time:
  One Hour
Preheat oven to 350°

- 4 oz. shrimp, peeled, deveined
- 2 whole eggs
- 1 egg yolk
- 1 tsp. Old Bay Seasoning
  Salt and pepper
- 1 cup heavy cream
- 2 lbs. fresh snapper bones
- 1 oz. sweet butter
- 5 cloves garlic, lightly crushed
- 5 large shallots, peeled, wrought out
- 1 Tbsp. ginger, chopped
- 2 celery stalks, ringed, diced
- 4 fresh lemon grass pieces, crushed
- 3 tsps. annatto seed powder*
- ½ bottle dry vermouth
- 2 cups chicken broth
- 2 cups heavy cream
- 1 cup coconut milk
- 8 oz. dry conch meat, cooked, chopped
- ½ bunch cilantro, finely chopped
  Olive oil for frying
- ½ tsp. vanilla powder
- 2 tsps. salt
  Pinch of cayenne pepper
- 1 medium yucca
  Grapeseed oil for frying

☆

Mango "Tarte Tatin" with Banana Ice Cream and Kumquat Aspic

Serves 4
Preparation Time:
 One Hour
(note refrigeration and
 freezing times)
Preheat oven to 400°

Ice Cream:

 1 cup heavy cream
 1 cup milk
 ½ vanilla bean
 1 cup ripe bananas
 9 egg yolks
 ½ cup + 1 Tbsp. sugar
 1 Tbsp. rum

Aspic:

 8 oz. sugar
 1 cup orange juice
 1 cup kumquat purée
 1 Tbsp. powdered
   gelatin

Tatin:

 Flour for rolling dough
 8 oz. pastry dough
 ¾ cup sugar
 2 large, firm ripe
   mangos, cut in wedges
 4 Tbsps. unsalted butter

In a heavy 3-quart non-reactive saucepan, combine the heavy cream and milk. Cut the vanilla bean half lengthwise, scrape, and add scrapings and bean halves to the pan. Bring to a boil.

Combine egg yolks and ½ cup sugar in a large bowl, whisking vigorously until thick and pale yellow, gradually add to the cream mixture, whisking constantly.

Return mixture to the saucepan and cook over medium heat, stirring constantly and scraping pan bottom evenly with a wooden spoon, just until it thickens and leaves a distinct trail on the back trail on the back of the spoon when you draw a finger through it. Do not let mixture boil.

Immediately strain through the chinois into the bowl. Promptly cover this custard cream and refrigerate until well chilled, approximately 2 hours.

When ready to finish the ice cream, combine the banana with remaining 1 Tbsp. sugar on a cutting board, kneading mixture with the back of a spoon until it becomes a paste. Add paste and rum to custard and mix vigorously.

Freeze in the ice cream machine according to manufacturer's instructions until firm, about 20 to 45 minutes.

For the aspic: Make a simple syrup by heating up in a sauce pan the sugar with the ¾ cup of orange juice. Let boil it for 1 minute. Let it cool and add the kumquat purée. Dissolve the gelatin in ¼ cup of orange juice (at room temperature) and add to the mixture. Let it cool in the refrigerator for 3 hours before using.

For the tatin: Place dough on a lightly floured surface and roll out a ⅛-inch thickness. Cut a 3½-inch round.

Place the round on a baking sheet lined with parchment paper and prick several times with a fork. Refrigerate for at least 1 hour.

Evenly distribute ½ cup of the sugar on the bottom of the skillet being used for the tatin. Cook over medium heat until sugar becomes a light caramel-colored syrup stirring constantly with a wooden spoon.

Remove skillet from the heat and carefully arrange the mango wedges inside all the way top of the skillet. Dot the top of the skillet with butter and sprinkle with ¼ cup sugar.

Remove the dough round from the refrigerator and arrange it evenly over the mango, pressing down edges to fit. Place skillet in a large baking pan. Bake until the crust is golden brown and cooked through, about 35 to 40 minutes. Remove from oven and let tatin cool for 5 minutes.

Invert a heat-proof serving platter over the skillet and while holding it very tight against the skillet top, quickly turn both over to unmold the tatin onto the platter. Let cool about 10 minutes.

To serve: Place the warm tatin the center of the plate, surrounding it with the kumquat aspic. Then top the tatin with a scoop of the banana ice cream and serve immediately.

Cooking Secret: Tarte Tatin is a famous French upside-down apple tart made by covering the bottom of a shallow baking dish with butter and sugar, then apples and finally a pastry crust, While baking, the sugar and butter create a delicious caramel that becomes the topping when the tart is inverted onto a serving plate. The tart was created by two French sisters who lived in the Loire Valley and earned their living making it. The French call this dessert tarte des demoiselles Tatin "the tart of two unmarried women named Tatin."

☆

IL TARTUFO ON LAS OLAS

CONTINENTAL CUISINE
2400 East Las Olas Boulevard
Fort Lauderdale, Florida 33301
(954) 767-9190
Open Daily Noon–11PM
Average Dinner for Two: $70

I l Tartufo is an oasis for hungry gourmets looking for classic Italian cuisine and live musical entertainment in one location. The Italian menu inspires a wide assortment of taste sensations.

Highlights include Carpaccio di Manzo Tartufato, a sliver-thin lean beef topped with fresh arugula, then lightly brushed with truffle oil and topped with Reggiano cheese. Risotto is a house specialty, as is the homemade pasta topped with fresh tomato-basil sauce.

There is something on the menu to please everyone—seafood as well as beef and rack of baby lamb. A delightful oak-roasted tender Long Island Duckling is cooked in Spicy Apricot Sauce, while Il Tartufo's Breast of Chicken is stuffed with Mushrooms, Spinach and Roasted Peppers, then smothered in a Port Wine Sauce. Delicious.

IL TARTUFO'S MENU FOR FOUR:

Risotto With Zucchini Flowers and Scallops

Yellowtail Snapper Filet in Clam Saffron Broth on a Bed of Steamed Escarole

Chestnut-Crusted Chicken Breast with Black Truffle Sauce

Risotto With Zucchini Flowers and Scallops

I n a medium-sized saucepan over low heat, put 2 Tbsps. olive oil. Add the shallot and sauté until golden brown. Add the white wine and cook until mixture is reduced. Set aside.

In a second medium-sized sauce pot, put the remaining 2 Tbsps. olive oil, garlic and onion and sauté over low heat until golden brown.

Add the rice, garlic and onion and mix together while adding the red wine. Constantly stir the rice. Begin adding the fish stock. Keep mixing until most of the liquid is absorbed.

Add the cooked scallops, parsley and reserved shallot.

Before serving, season to taste with salt and pepper, add the butter and top with the zucchini flowers.

Serves 4
Preparation Time:
  45 Minutes

  4 Tbsps. extra-virgin olive oil
  1 Tbsp. shallot, chopped
  1 cup white wine
  1 Tbsp. garlic, sliced
  1 Tbsp. Bermuda onion, chopped
  2 cups arborio rice
  ¼ cup red wine
  4 cups fish stock
 20 sea scallops, cooked
  1 Tbsp. Italian parsley, chopped
     Salt and pepper to taste
  1 Tbsp. butter
  1 cup zucchini flowers

★

Yellowtail Snapper Filet in Clam Saffron Broth on a Bed of Steamed Escarole

Serves 4
Preparation Time:
  15 Minutes

  1 Tbsp. extra-virgin olive
    oil
  4 yellowtail snapper
    filets
    Pinch of saffron
  1 Tbsp. chives, chopped
  ¼ cup Chardonnay wine
 48 littleneck clams
  ¼ cup clam juice
  1 head of escarole or
    endive
    Salt and pepper to
    taste

n a large sauté pan, put the olive oil and heat. Place the snapper filets in the hot oil and sauté until cooked through.

Add the saffron, chives, wine, clams and clam juice. Keeping on low heat, cover and let steam for about 5 minutes.

In a pot of boiling water, cook the escarole for 1 minute. Then remove and strain. Cool and slice into wedges.

Sauté the escarole quickly in oil until heated through. Season to taste with salt and pepper.

To serve, place wedges of the escarole on serving plates and top with the snapper filets.

☆

Chestnut-Crusted Chicken Breast with Black Truffle Sauce

n a large skillet, heat 2 Tbsps. olive oil. Sauté the chicken breasts until browned on all sides. Remove from heat.

In a food processor, grind the chestnuts with ½ cup olive. Coat the browned chicken breasts with the chestnut mixture.

Return the chicken breasts to the skillet. Add the wine, chicken broth and black truffle. Bring to high heat and reduce sauce for 5 minutes. Add butter and stir. Cover tightly, reduce heat and cook until just tender. This will take anywhere from 10 to 20 minutes, depending on the size of the chicken breasts.

To serve, place a chicken breast on each serving plate and drizzle the sauce over it.

Cooking Secret: The ideal vegetable accompaniments for this dish are roasted long-wedged potatoes and sautéed Swiss chard.

Serves 4
Preparation Time:
 20 Minutes

¾ cup olive oil
4 chicken breasts, 6 oz. each
¼ lb. fresh chestnuts
½ cup white wine
1 cup chicken broth
1 black truffle, chopped
1 tsp. butter

☆

NORMAN'S

NEW WORLD CUISINE
21 Almeria Avenue
Coral Gables, Florida 33134
(305) 446-6767
Lunch Monday–Friday Noon–2PM
Dinner Monday–Saturday 6PM–10:30PM
Average Dinner for Two: $55

From his pioneering work in Key West in the early 1980s, chef/owner/cookbook author Norman Van Aken is acknowledged as the originator of South Florida's vibrant "New World Cuisine." His menus reflect cultural diversity, celebrating Latin America and the Caribbean, with touches of Asia and fresh native gems of papayas, kumquats, mangoes and pineapples. Both his restaurant and cuisine have been applauded by the James Beard Foundation, Bon Appetit magazine and Condé Nast, to name a few.

Some of his mouth-watering signature dishes are the Vegetarian Vietnamese Soft Spring Rolls with Ponzu and Crushed Peanut-Shoyu Salsa, Crab Cakes topped with West Indian Guacamole, Lobster and Shrimp Risotto with Roasted Peppers, Fennel, Leeks and Oven-Dried Tomatoes and wood-oven Roasted Chicken surrounded by Black Beans, accompanied with homemade Mango Chutney. The mix of flavors is a delight to the senses.

NORMAN'S MENU FOR FOUR:

White Bean, Chorizo and Collard Green Caldo Gallego

Cracked Conch with Banana Butter and Red Onion Citrus Salsa

Key Lime Cheesecake with Toasted Nut Crust

White Bean, Chorizo and Collard Green Caldo Gallego

Cover white beans with water and soak overnight. Heat a large, heavy soup pot over medium heat and add the olive oil. Once it is warm, lay the chorizo sausage in the pan and turn it as necessary to brown. Pierce the sausage casing in a few places with the tip of a small knife. Lower the heat to low and cook the sausage 10 to 12 minutes and then remove it to a plate. Allow to cool a few minutes and then put it in the refrigerator to firm up.

Working in the same soup pot, melt the butter over medium heat. Add the garlic, Scotch bonnet and poblano chiles and the red onion. Allow to cook 7 to 8 minutes, stirring only occasionally.

Drain the soaking beans and add them to the pan. Stir well. Add the chicken stock, the pork hock and the bay leaves. Turn up the heat and bring it to just under a boil, skimming as necessary. Turn the heat to low and add the beef chuck. Do not cover. Stir occasionally, checking to make sure the beans don't become stuck to the bottom of the pan.

When the beans are almost tender, season them with a pinch of salt and pepper. Add the potato, turnip and collard greens. Cook until the potato is just tender, about 45 minutes.

Remove the chorizo from the refrigerator. Cut it into $\frac{1}{2}$-inch rounds and add it to the soup. Shred the beef when it is done enough and return it to the soup.

Season to taste and serve.

Serves 8
Preparation Time:
  1¼ hours
(note soaking time)

1½ cups dried white
  beans, rinsed, picked
  over
3 Tbsps. pure olive oil
8 oz. chorizo or other
  spicy sausage
2 Tbsps. butter
6 cloves garlic, peeled,
  sliced thin
2 Scotch bonnet chiles,
  stemmed, seeded,
  minced
2 poblano chiles,
  stemmed, seeded,
  minced
1 medium red onion,
  peeled, diced
3 qts. chicken stock
1 smoked pork hock
  and ham bone
2 bay leaves, broken
½ lb. beef chuck steak,
  left in one piece,
  rubbed with black
  pepper
  Salt and pepper to
  taste
1 red potato, diced
1 turnip, diced
2 cups collard greens,
  stemmed, shredded

★

Cracked Conch with Banana Butter and Red Onion Citrus Salsa

Serves 4
Preparation Time:
45 Minutes

1 lb. conch
½ tsp. sea salt
½ Tbsp. black pepper
½ tsp. cayenne
2 eggs, beaten
2 Tbsps. water
¼ cup flour
12 oz. fine kataifi*
Canola oil for sautéing
Banana Butter (recipe follows)
Red Onion Citrus Salsa (recipe follows)

Cut the conch into 2- to 3-oz. pieces on a strong bias. Place each slice, one at a time, in between two sheets of plastic wrap and pound until it is almost paper-thin, but not falling apart.

Mix together the salt, pepper and cayenne. Season the conch with it. Make an egg wash with the beaten eggs and water.

Dip the conch in the flour, then the egg wash and lastly spread some of the kataifi on both sides of each piece. Set aside on a large platter, layering it with wax paper so the conch doesn't stick together.

Heat one or two large sauté pans over medium high heat. Add the canola oil. Add the conch pieces and allow them to brown nicely on both sides. When all the conch is cooked, spoon some of the plantain butter toward the outer areas of 4 hot plates. Now arrange the cooked conch in the center of the plates. Scatter the citrus salsa evenly over the plantain butter. Serve.

* Kataifi is a Middle Eastern shredded phyllo product now becoming more widely available.

Cooking Secret: The richness of the plantain butter calls for a simple green vegetable dish. Chef Van Aken likes sautéed spinach, asparagus or grilled chayote.

★

Red Onion Citrus Salsa

Heat a skillet over medium-high heat. Add the extra virgin olive oil and the butter. When the butter melts, toss in the diced red onion and season with the salt and pepper and stir once. Don't stir too often, but allow the onion to char on the edges. When they are nicely colored, add the reserved citrus juices and reduce them with the onions until very little liquid remains.

Remove the onions to a bowl and allow to cool to room temperature.

Cut the reserved fruit into medium-small dice and reserve in a cool place. Do not combine the onions and the citrus until ready to serve.

- ½ Tbsp. olive oil
- ½ Tbsp. butter
- ½ red onion, peeled, diced medium-small
- Salt and pepper to taste
- 1 orange, peeled, sectioned, juice reserved, sections reserved covered in the refrigerator
- 1 Mandarin orange, peeled, sectioned, juice reserved
- 1 ruby grapefruit, peeled, sectioned, juice reserved
- 1 blood orange, peeled, sectioned, juice reserved (optional)

☆

Banana Butter

Heat a heavy, small saucepan. Add the butter and allow to foam. With the heat on medium-high, add the plantain pieces and allow them to turn golden on one side. Add the shallots and then turn the plantain pieces over once. Stir the plantain-shallot mixture occasionally and allow the plantain's natural sugars to come to the surface and get nice and dark.

Scrape the seeds of the vanilla bean into the pan. Toss in the bean as well. Roughly mash the plantain to give it full flavor. Add the vinegar. Immediately add ¼ cup of the heavy cream and as soon as it boils, whisk in the butter, piece by piece. When all of the butter is incorporated, strain the mixture through a medium-mesh strainer into a warm bowl (push down the mixture with your whisk to squeeze it out). Try to get a lot of the vanilla seeds into the reserved butter. Discard the solids. Add the remaining warm heavy cream. Season to taste.

Keep the butter in a warm place until ready to serve.

- 2 Tbsps. butter
- ½ very ripe plantain, peeled, cut into ¼-inch sections
- 2 shallots, peeled, thinly sliced
- ½ vanilla bean, cut in half lengthwise
- 2 Tbsps. champagne vinegar
- ½ cup heavy cream
- ½ lb. butter, cut into small pieces, kept cold
- Salt, pepper and cayenne to taste

☆

Key Lime Cheesecake with Toasted Nut Crust

Yield: One 10-inch cheesecake
Preparation Time: 1½ Hours
Preheat oven to 350°

1 cup graham cracker crumbs
¾ cup almonds or any nuts you prefer, toasted, ground
⅓ cup sugar
1 tsp. cinnamon
1 tsp. nutmeg
⅓ cup sweet butter, melted
Key lime filling (recipe follows)

n a mixing bowl, combine the graham cracker crumbs, nuts, sugar, cinnamon, nutmeg and melted butter. Press crust mixture firmly into a 10-inch springform pan.

Pour the filling into the crust. Bake at 350° for 1 hour.

Remove from the oven and run a thin knife around the mold to loosen the cheesecake. Release the springform pan and cool the cheesecake.

Cooking Secret: Chef Van Aken recommends serving this cheesecake with a coulis of fresh berries and an espresso.

☆

Key Lime Cheesecake Filling

Cream the cream cheese, sugar, egg yolks, sour cream, vanilla extract and Key lime juice in an electric mixer, adding one item at a time.

In a separate bowl, beat the egg whites until barely stiff. Fold into the cream cheese mixture.

Cooking Secret: Key limes are another facet of recipes that distinguish New World Cuisine. What is not widely known is that the Key lime is the true lime, while the green Tahitian limes are really an anomalous hybrid of lemon.

1 lb. cream cheese
¾ cup sugar
4 egg yolks
1 cup sour cream
½ tsp. pure vanilla extract
¼ cup Key lime juice
4 egg whites

☆

St. George and the Dragon

CONTINENTAL CUISINE
936 Fifth Avenue South
Naples, Florida 34102
(941) 262-6546
Lunch Monday–Saturday 11AM–4PM
Dinner Monday–Saturday 4:30PM–10PM
Average Dinner for Two: $75

R are marine antiques, hand-carved wooden beams and softly lit brass lamps greet you upon your arrival at this Naples landmark restaurant. Since 1969, the hearty fare, consistent in quality, has been a favorite of Neapolitans and visitors alike. The service is excellent, with a wait staff that is knowledgeable and experienced.

Starters range from Soft-Shell Crabs Sautéed in Butter to marvelous French Snails in their Shells with Wine, Garlic, Butter and Herbs and Conch Chowder with a touch of sherry. The "Cattleman's" extra-thick Sirloin is a full 22 ounces of incomparable aged, center-cut strip steak, done to perfection.

ST. GEORGE AND THE DRAGON'S MENU FOR FOUR:

Cream of Roasted Red Pepper Soup

Goat Cheese-Crusted Rack of Lamb

Onion Rings

Cream of Roasted Red Pepper Soup

Sauté the peppers and onion in a small amount of olive oil or butter in a heavy-bottomed saucepan over medium-low heat. Cook until the onion is well cooked and soft—do not allow it to brown. Season with white pepper and thyme and cook for 1 minute more.

Add the chicken stock and bring to a boil. Allow to cool slightly, then purée in food processor or blender until smooth.

Pour into a bowl and add cream to taste.

Chill until very cold. Pour into chilled bowls and garnish with minced chives before serving.

Serves 6
Preparation Time:
30 Minutes

4 large red bell peppers, roasted, peeled, seeded
1 medium onion, julienned
2 Tbsps. olive oil or butter
½ tsp. white pepper
1 tsp. dried thyme
1 cup chicken stock
1 to 1½ cups heavy cream
Chives, minced for garnish

Goat Cheese-Crusted Rack of Lamb

Serves 4
Preparation Time:
45 Minutes
(note marinating time)
Preheat oven to 425°

¼ cup olive oil
¼ cup onion, chopped
¼ cup celery, chopped
¼ cup carrots, chopped
½ cup garlic cloves,
  mashed
2 Tbsps. dried rosemary
2 Tbsps. dried basil
2 Tbsps. dried oregano
½ cup balsamic vinegar
¼ cup Dijon mustard
½ cup Worcestershire
  sauce
1 cup red wine
1 Tbsp. black pepper
  Salt to taste
4 racks of lamb, 10 to
  12 oz. each, frenched
6 oz. goat cheese, at
  room temperature
2 Tbsps. shallots, minced
1 Tbsp. garlic, minced
4 Tbsps. assorted fresh
  herbs such as
  rosemary, thyme,
  oregano, chives
1 Tbsp. salt
1 Tbsp. black pepper
1 cup fresh bread
  crumbs
¼ cup butter, melted

Heat oil in a large skillet over medium-high heat. Add the vegetables and sauté until they start to soften, about 8 minutes. Add the garlic cloves and herbs and sauté for 2 minutes. Add the vinegar, mustard, Worcestershire sauce, red wine and pepper and bring to a boil. Season to taste with salt. Remove and allow to cool to room temperature.

Place lamb racks in a non-reactive container and pour marinade over them. Allow to marinate for 4 hours.

Heat a grill until hot. Remove lamb from marinade and towel dry with paper towels. Brush with olive oil and sprinkle with a small amount of salt. Sear lamb on both sides, about 2 minutes per side.

In a small mixing bowl, combine the goat cheese, shallots, garlic, herbs, salt and pepper. Mix until smooth.

Using a pastry brush, brush the goat cheese mixture onto the lamb. Place the bread crumbs in a shallow pan and press the crumbs onto the lamb to form a thin coating. Drizzle with melted butter.

Remove to a baking dish and place in a preheated 425° oven until desired doneness is achieved, about 12 minutes for medium. Remove from the oven and allow to rest for 5 minutes before carving.

Onion Rings

Peel onions and slice into very thin rings. Lay rings in a single layer on a pan lined with paper towels. Sprinkle with salt and refrigerate.

Heat oil in a deep, heavy stock pot to 375°. Lightly dust the onion rings with flour and shake to remove any excess.

Drop into hot oil and fry until golden brown and crisp. Stir constantly once you drop the onions into the oil to prevent them from sticking together.

Remove from the oil onto a paper-lined plate and sprinkle with salt. Serve warm.

Serves 4
Preparation Time:
   15 Minutes
(note refrigeration time)

2 **sweet onions**
   Salt to taste
2 **qts. canola oil for**
   frying
   Flour for dusting

VITO'S WATERFRONT

ITALIAN CUISINE
1079 Bald Eagle Drive
Marco Island, Florida 34145
(941) 394-7722
Web Site: www.vitos.com
Open Daily Lunch and Dinner
Average Dinner for Two: $60

C reative Italian cuisine, mouthwatering steaks and the freshest seafood around are enjoyed in this waterfront dining establishment with an outside deck overlooking the Marcos River. Adjacent to the marina, Vito's Waterfront serves lunch and dinner, accompanied by live jazz.

A recent recipient of the Wine Spectator '96 and '97 awards of excellence for more than 200 wines, Vito's offers selections from the United States, Italy, France, Germany, Australia and Chile.

Tempting menu favorites are Salmon Parmesan encrusted with Parmesan cheese, Italian herbs and bread crumbs, pan-seared and served over fettuccine pasta that has been gently tossed with sun-dried tomato and basil pesto. The Caribbean Conch Chowder is prepared "down under" style, with dark rum. Absolutely a "must try."

VITO'S WATERFRONT MENU FOR FOUR:

Portobello Marsala

Warm Asparagus Salad with Artichoke and Balsamic Vinaigrette

Salmon Parmesan

Portobello Marsala

R inse and remove the stems of the mushrooms from the caps and set aside. Leave the caps whole.

Sauté the caps of the mushrooms in a sauté pan with ¼ cup olive oil, bottom-side first, until golden brown. Flip and turn off flame.

In a different sauté pan, add ¼ cup olive oil and heat. Add the garlic, sun-dried tomatoes and diced mushroom stems. Sauté quickly and flame with Marsala wine.

Add the butter and veal demi-glace. Heat for 3 minutes over medium heat.

Add the cooked pasta and toss. Place in the center of a large dinner plate.

Remove caps from the sauté pan and cut them on the bias and fan out over the center of the pasta. Garnish with fresh, chopped parsley.

Serves 4
Preparation Time:
   15 Minutes

16 large portobello
    mushrooms
½ cup olive oil
¼ cup garlic, diced
½ lb. sun-dried tomatoes
 1 cup Marsala wine
12 Tbsps. (1½ sticks)
    whole butter
 3 cups veal demi-glace
    or veal stock
 1 lb. angel hair pasta,
    cooked
    Parsley, chopped, for
    garnish

☆

Warm Asparagus Salad with Artichoke and Balsamic Vinaigrette

Serves 4
Preparation Time:
   15 Minutes

   1 lb. baby salad mix
   4 small plum tomatoes, diced
   2 small red onions, diced
   1 garlic clove, finely diced
   4 artichokes, medium-sized, cooked and quartered
  16 medium-length asparagus spears, cooked, chilled for garnish

Balsamic Vinaigrette
Yield: 1 cup

   ¼ cup fresh basil, chopped
   ¼ cup balsamic vinegar
   ¾ cup extra-virgin olive oil
   ½ tsp. Dijon mustard

I n a salad bowl, combine the salad mix with the tomatoes, onions, garlic and artichokes. Set aside.

For the vinaigrette, combine the basil, vinegar, olive oil and mustard in a blender and emulsify. Pour into a sauté pan and bring the vinaigrette to a simmer.

Pour the vinaigrette over the greens and toss quickly. Top the salad with the chilled asparagus spears and serve.

☆

Salmon Parmesan

or the basil pesto combine the basil leaves, 1 cup pine nuts, 2 garlic cloves and 2 cups oil in a food processor and purée to form a pesto. Set aside.

For the sun-dried tomato pesto combine the tomatoes, 1 cup pine nuts, 2 garlic cloves, 1 cup oil, salt and pepper to taste in a food processor and purée. Set aside.

Mix the Parmesan cheese with the bread crumbs in a large bowl or on a plate. Set aside.

Place the salmon in the flour, shake off extra flour and dip in the egg wash, then dip in the Parmesan breading.

Sauté lightly in an oven-proof sauté pan with olive oil, browning lightly on both sides, then place in the oven at 300°. Cook to medium, about 5 to 10 minutes.

Toss the cooked pasta with the two pestos, the vermouth and the butter.

Serve salmon over pasta and garnish with freshly chopped parsley.

Serves 4
Preparation Time:
45 Minutes
Preheat oven to 300°

3 cups basil leaves, roughly chopped
2 cups pine nuts, toasted
4 garlic cloves, sliced
3 cups olive oil
1½ lbs. sun-dried tomatoes
Salt and pepper to taste
1 cup Parmesan cheese, grated
3 cups fine Italian bread crumbs
4 fresh salmon filets, 8 oz. each
2 cups flour, seasoned with salt and pepper
3 eggs, beaten
2 Tbsps. olive oil
1 lb. egg fettuccine pasta, cooked
1 cup vermouth
12 Tbsps. (1½ sticks) whole butter
Parsley, chopped, for garnish

ALBION HOTEL

1650 James Avenue at Lincoln Road
Miami Beach, Florida 33139
(888) 665-0008
(305) 913-1000
Web Site: www.albion.com
Room Rates: $100–$1,000

In the heart of Miami Beach's Art Deco District stands the Albion Hotel. This 1939 masterpiece originally designed by Igor Polevitzky, renowned architect of Havana's Hotel Nacional, is a showpiece for avant garde architecture. Under the guidance of Ecuadorian architect Carlos Zapata, the hotel reopened in 1997 after a $10 million historical renovation. Every guest room was custom-designed with both comfort and visual stimulation in mind. The rooms feature a unique line of postmodern furnishings and accessories designed exclusively for the Albion. Most also feature king-sized beds, and all the modern amenities.

In the hotel lobby, guests are greeted by a 500-square-foot vertical pond. The courtyard has portholes that look directly into the swimming pool.

The Fallaballa Bar was named the "Best New Bar in Miami" by the New Times.

Yellow Gazpacho

ix all ingredients together and marinate for 24 hours in the refrigerator. Serve chilled.

Serves 6
Preparation Time:
  5 Minutes
(note marinating time)

12 yellow tomatoes, seeded
2 cucumbers, seedless
2 yellow pepper
2 small yellow onion
3 Tbsps. rice wine vinegar
  Salt and pepper to taste
  Cilantro to taste
  Parsley to taste

BOCA RATON RESORT AND CLUB

501 East Camino Real
P.O. Box 5025
Boca Raton, Florida 33431
(800) 327-0101
(407) 395-3000
Room Rates: $113–$1,100

Boca Raton Resort and Club is a stylish place to play. The resort has been ranked among the finest in the country for golf and tennis. Guests can enjoy a variety of nautical fun such as windsurfing, snorkeling, sailing and yacht charters.

This 356-acre estate is decorated by nature with brilliant tropical flowers and exotic birds, set off by historic architecture. Each of the different accommodations has its own unique style. The Cloister rooms are Mediterranean charm, grace and elegance. The Tower rooms are contemporary and cosmopolitan and rise 27 stories above the Intracoastal Waterway. The Golf Villas are spacious and secluded, nestled within the resort golf course. The Boca Raton Beach Club rooms are more casual and comfortable, directly on the private beach.

Florida Citrus Mojo Turkey

One day in advance, rinse turkey inside and out with water. Pat dry. Loosen the skin from the breast, thighs and drumsticks by sliding your fingers underneath the skin. Rub salt and pepper under skin. Place ½ cup of garlic evenly under the skin. Arrange the orange slices evenly under the skin. Season with salt, pepper and remaining garlic. Cover with plastic and refrigerate overnight.

Melt the butter over medium heat in a sauté pan. Add the cumin, oregano, lime juice and salt and pepper. Remove turkey from the refrigerator. Tie the ends of the legs to the tail with a cord. Lift wing tips up and over the back and tuck them under the bird.

Place turkey on roasting rack, breast side up. Brush entire bird generously with the butter mixture inside and out. Roast the bird at 325° for 2½ to 3 hours. Baste the bird every 20 minutes with the pan drippings. The skin will become golden brown and the leg juices will run clear when pricked with a skewer. If a meat thermometer is used, it should read 185°.

Transfer the turkey to a platter or cutting board. Let stand 30 minutes before carving. Strain the pan drippings and serve in a sauce boat on the side.

Cooking Secret: One tip for roasting the perfect turkey is to baste your bird throughout the cooking process for perfect color. Always cook the turkey in one continuous cooking period or the meat will toughen; never allow the turkey to thaw at room temperature—always thaw under refrigeration.

Serves 6
Preparation Time:
  3 Hours
(note marinating time)
Preheat oven to 325°

1 turkey, 12 to 14 lbs.
  Salt and pepper to
  taste
1 cup garlic cloves, cut
  into slivers
1 orange, sliced thin
½ cup unsalted butter
2 tsps. ground cumin
2 tsps. fresh oregano,
  chopped
1 cup lime juice

CHESTERFIELD HOTEL

363 Cocoanut Row
Palm Beach, Florida 33480
(800) 243-7871
(561) 659-5800
Room Rates: $89–$1,099

Located in the heart of Palm Beach, just off Worth Avenue, is the historic four-star Chesterfield Hotel. The elegant surroundings are an impressive blend of modern conveniences with the gracious standards of the Third Earl of Chesterfield and the hotel, offers an uncompromised level of comfort and service.

The beautifully appointed accommodations have distinctive styles, specially chosen fabrics, elegant furnishings and deluxe marble bathrooms. Amenities include plush dressing robes, fine soaps, bottled mineral water and 24-hour room service.

An English tea fit for a queen is prepared by the executive chef every afternoon. Fashionable dining and gourmet meals are a specialty of the hotel's theater-style kitchen, where each of the culinary experts creates outstanding cuisine for all tastes. The Leopard Room and Lounge is an exotic, playful nightspot combining luxury, leisure and entertainment.

The Chesterfield Hotel is located only three short blocks from the beach. The hotel's heated swimming pool, spa and private cabaña offer you a tropical setting in which to relax from dusk 'til dawn.

Jamaican Shrimp

P urée all of the above ingredients except the shrimp and the butter in a food processor until smooth.

Use ½ of this purée to marinade the shrimp, tossing with marinade in a bowl. Place the bowl with the shrimp and marinade in the refrigerator for 2 hours.

It is best to use a large, very hot cast iron skillet for cooking the shrimp. Lightly oil the skillet and add the shrimp until the pan is smoky hot. Do not overcrowd the shrimp, as that will take away from the charring effect. Toss the shrimp in the pan until they are cooked thoroughly. Remove the shrimp from the skillet and keep hot.

Using the same skillet, add the remaining puréed ingredients and the butter. Remove from the heat and stir until a sauce forms. Pour the sauce over the seared shrimp and serve.

Cooking Secret: This dish goes well with any type of rice or greens.

Serves 8
Preparation Time:
  30 Minutes
(note marinating time)

  1 medium yellow onion,
    peeled, coarsely diced
  4 cloves garlic
  3 scallions
  1 red bell pepper, cored,
    coarsely diced
  1 jalapeño pepper,
    seeded
    Juice of 1 lime
  ¼ cup soy sauce
  2 Tbsps. ginger root,
    chopped
1½ Tbsps. sugar
  1 Tbsp. fresh thyme,
    chopped
  1 Tbsp. fresh cilantro,
    chopped
  1 cup olive oil
  1 Tbsp. mace
  ½ Tbsp. cinnamon
  2 tsps. black pepper
  2 tsps. salt
 32 large fresh shrimp,
    peeled, deveined,
    with tails attached
  ½ lb. soft butter

★

Boundary Waters Stuffed Chicken

Serves 8
Preparation Time:
  35 Minutes
Preheat oven to 375°

  10 boneless chicken
      breasts, 7-8 oz. each
   1 egg white
  ¾ cup wild rice, cooked
   1 cup shiitake
      mushrooms, coarsely
      chopped
  ¼ cup dried cranberries,
      optional
   2 tsps. salt
   2 tsps. black pepper
  ½ Tbsp. fresh sage,
      chopped
  ½ Tbsp. fresh thyme,
      chopped
   1 cup heavy cream
   1 oz. olive oil
   2 shallots, chopped
   3 cloves garlic, chopped
   1 cup Madeira
   4 cups chicken stock

P repare 8 of the chicken breasts for stuffing, with skin side down. Using a sharp knife, butterfly the breasts to create a cavity for stuffing. Spread the open breasts on a sheet pan and refrigerate.

Remove the skin and any remaining fat from the 2 remaining breasts. Using a food processor, purée the 2 breasts with the egg white until a smooth paste forms.

Transfer the paste to a chilled, stainless-steel bowl containing the wild rice, mushrooms, cranberries, salt, pepper, sage and thyme.

Using a rubber spatula, fold in the heavy cream in 3 to 4 sessions, blending the ingredients thoroughly until the cream is well absorbed.

With the butterflied breasts spread out, evenly fill each one with the mousse. Fold the meat around the stuffing to seal, leaving no mousse exposed. Secure the folded breast with butcher's twine.

In large pan, sear the stuffed breasts in olive oil until the skin is rendered golden brown. Remove the chicken and set aside.

In the same pan, sweat the shallots, add garlic and Madeira wine. Simmer for 10 seconds and add chicken stock. Reduce to half.

Put seared breasts back in the pan and bake in oven for 25 minutes. Remove butcher's twine. Pour the sauce from the pan over the breasts and serve whole or sliced for presentation.

Semolina Cake with Fruit Compote

For the cake: Lightly whip butter until creamed. Add all other ingredients and whip until smooth. Transfer to a greased 9-inch round cake pan.

Bake for 25 minutes. Let cool.

For the compote: In sauce pot or large sauté pan, over medium heat, add brown sugar, Grand Marnier, cloves, pears, apples and water. Cook until fruit is tender.

Add all other ingredients. Let simmer 3 to 4 minutes. Strain liquid into a thick gauge sauce pot. Set aside.

Place pot with strained liquid from the fruit compote over medium heat. Add sugar, water, lemon juice and cinnamon.

Let simmer without stirring until reduced to the consistency of syrup. Remove from heat.

Serve warm, soaked into slices of semolina cake with compote garnish on top. Add whipped cream on top.

Serves 8
Preparation Time:
 30 Minutes
Preheat oven to 350°

Cake:

 ½ cup soft butter
 ½ cup sugar
  Juice and rind of
  1 orange
 ¾ cup semolina
 ¼ cup all-purpose flour
 1 Tbsp. baking powder

Fruit Compote:

 3 Tbsps. brown sugar
 2 oz. Grand Marnier
 3 whole cloves
 1 fresh pear, peeled,
  diced
 2 green apples, peeled,
  diced
 3 Tbsps. water
 ¼ cup raisins
 ½ cup cherries, fresh
  pitted or maraschino
 ¼ cup pecans, toasted
 1 cup sugar
 2 cups water
  Juice of 1 lemon
 2 cinnamon sticks
  Whipped cream for
  garnish

☆

EDEN ROC RESORT AND SPA

4525 Collins Avenue
Miami Beach, Florida 33140
(888) EDEN ROC
(800) 327-8337
(305) 531-0000
Web Site: www.edenrocresort.com
Room Rates: $129–$1,500

The majestic, 14-story Eden Roc, the largest oceanfront spa in the country, offers 350 luxurious rooms and suites and has been ranked as one of the best of the best by "Fitness Magazine."

All accommodations feature magnificent ocean and/or bay views. Some offer spacious private balconies. Every room boasts exquisite Italian marble baths with colorful mosaic tile accents, top quality linens and mini-bars.

You will enjoy two heated swimming pools and private poolside cabanas, each with telephone and television. A glass-enclosed weight room, overlooking both pools and the ocean, features state-of-the-art equipment. The Spa of Eden also boasts an indoor Sport Club, which features South Florida's only rock-climbing arena, basketball court, squash and racquetball. Personal services include a full array of massage therapies and body treatments. Guests can enjoy the use of steamroom, sauna, Swiss showers and pools.

Tropical Floribbean Shrimp

Cook the pasta according to directions, adding the saffron to the boiling water. Set aside.

Heat a skillet and add oil to coat. Add the shrimp and garlic. Slowly add the sherry and deglaze. Cook for 2 to 3 minutes or until the shrimp is almost done. Add the remaining ingredients and sauté until heated through.

Reheat pasta and add to the mixture in the skillet. Toss.

Arrange on plate and garnish with the portobello mushroom.

Serves 2
Preparation Time:
  15 Minutes

- ½ lb. angel hair pasta
- 3 pinches of saffron
- 2 Tbsps. vegetable oil
- 8 medium shrimp, peeled, deveined
- 1 clove garlic, peeled
- 2 Tbsps. dry sherry
- ½ kiwi, diced
- ½ cup fresh papaya, diced
- 1 plum tomato, diced
- ½ cup sweet butter, melted
  Salt and pepper to taste
- 1 portobello mushroom, sliced, grilled, for garnish

★

GROVE ISLE CLUB AND RESORT

4 Grove Isle Drive
Coconut Grove, Florida 33133
(800) 88-GROVE
(305) 858-8300
Room Rates: $168–$600

T he ultimate in relaxed, tropical elegance, Grove Isle Club and Resort is situated on its own secluded island, making it one of the most private and hospitable retreats in Florida. The island's 85-slip private marina is home to some of Miami's finest watercraft. Sunset cruises, sailing charters and deep-sea fishing excursions are only some of the activities guests can choose.

Each of the guest rooms and suites boasts a private terrace with floor-to-ceiling windows that look out to Miami's waterfront and cityscape. The rooms are furnished with tropical pastels, blond mahogany furnishings, original artwork and imported marble.

Fine dining is the standard at Grove Isle Club and Resort. The highly acclaimed gourmet restaurant offers eclectic cuisine with superior indoor and outdoor dining.

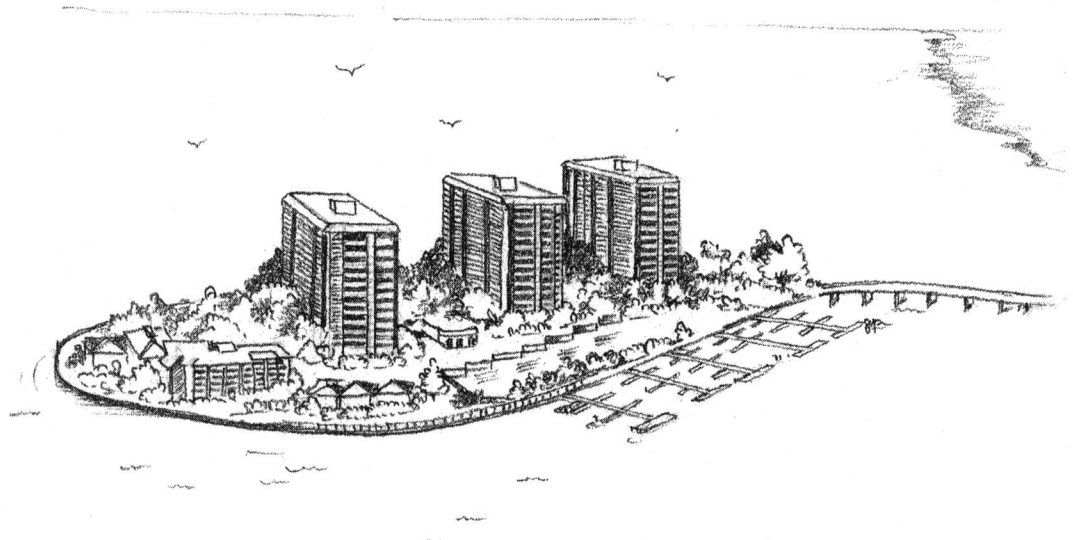

Garlic-Stuffed Tenderloin of Beef with Porcini Sauce

Remove all the fat and silvery skin from the filets. Cut a slit in the side of the filets and set aside.

Prepare the garlic by leaving it whole and unpeeled and rubbing it with oil, salt and pepper. Place in an oven at 300° and cook for 40 minutes. Cut the top off the garlic and squeeze sides until the garlic comes out. Place the roasted garlic into the slit in the filets. Season with salt and pepper and place on grill.

In a saucepan, put the shallots and carrots. Sauté until brown. Deglaze with red wine and reduce by half. Add demiglace and let sauce reduce again by half. Add thyme. Strain. Save sauce to complete dish.

In another pot, reconstitute porcini mushrooms in wine for approximately 10 minutes. Drain. Chop mushrooms and add to sauce.

In a food processor, purée sun-dried tomatoes, capers, anchovies, olives, olive oil, pepper, garlic salt and lemon juice into a paste.

Grill filets to desired doneness. Top with tapenade and pour porcini sauce over all. Serve with French beans, scalloped potatoes or sugar snap beans.

Serves 2
Preparation Time:
 35 Minutes
Preheat oven to 300°

2 tenderloin filets, 8 oz. each
2 cloves garlic
 Oil
 Salt and pepper to taste
1 cup shallots, sliced
3 carrots, sliced
1 cup red wine
3 cups demi-glace
¼ bunch thyme
1 cup dried porcini mushrooms
1 cup sun-dried tomatoes
3 Tbsps. capers
3 anchovy filets
½ cups olives, pitted
 Olive oil
 Pepper to taste
 Garlic salt to taste
2 Tbsps. garlic, chopped
2 Tbsps. lemon juice

☆

La Casa Del Mar

3003 Granada Street
Fort Lauderdale, Florida 33304
(800) 739-0009
(954) 467-2037
Web Site: www.lacasadelmar.com
E-mail: la-casa@travelbase.com
Room Rates: $75–$135

L a Casa del Mar, a charming, two-story Spanish Mediterranean-style bed and breakfast, is the area's most quaint and private inn, just 300 feet from the beach. Each of the spacious guest rooms is decorated with the owners' personal treasures and offers a private bath, air conditioning, VCR and refrigerator. Guests can choose from different rooms such as Stolen Kiss, Monet or the Southwest rooms.

In the serenity of the tropical gardens, around the fountain, enjoy a full American breakfast featuring orange French toast, poached eggs and crêpes, homemade breads and coffee cakes, herbal teas and hazelnut coffee. Afternoon wine and cheese parties are included in your room rate as well.

Baked Artichoke Dip

Mix all ingredients together in a bowl. Pour into an attractive baking dish. Sprinkle with cayenne pepper and parsley flakes. Bake at 350° for 30 to 45 minutes. The dip needs to be hot and bubbly.

Serve in the baking dish with nacho chips, crackers or vegetables.

Serves 8
Preparation Time:
 45 Minutes
Preheat oven to 350°

2 cups mayonnaise
2 cloves garlic, mashed
2 cups Parmesan cheese, grated
2 medium cans artichoke hearts
Dash of Worcestershire sauce
Cayenne pepper to taste
Parsley flakes to taste

Lago Mar Resort and Club

1700 South Ocean Lane
Fort Lauderdale, Florida 33316
(800) 255-5246
(954) 523-6511
Room Rates: $180–$415

Nestled between Lake Mayan and the Atlantic Ocean, Lago Mar Resort and Club feels more like an island. Guests are minutes away from downtown Fort Lauderdale yet have a private sandy beach at their disposal.

Some guests enjoy a drink from the Promenade bar while relaxing by the Swimming Lagoon. The Lagoon has its own mini-tropical island with palm trees to sit and relax under. Tennis buffs enjoy the option of lake-view or oceanfront courts. The miniature golf course, shuffleboard or beach-front volleyball are fun ways to loll away the days.

The different restaurants are each worth trying. The outdoor Sea Grape Terrace overlooks the lagoon pool and beach while the Palm Garden Room is more formal with dancing nightly.

Seafood Strudel

Blanch the bay scallops, crab meat and shrimp.
In a bowl, mix together cream cheese, white pepper, Old Bay Seasoning, dill, lemon juice, lobster base and sherry wine. Mix well. Lightly fold in all seafood.

Butter each layer of the phyllo dough sheets, lightly butter each layer. Place 4 oz. of seafood mix in the short side of the phyllo dough and roll over the dough one time leaving 1 inch on each side of dough with no seafood between it. Lightly butter the 1 inch ends. Fold ends into the middle. Lightly butter the rest of the top side of the dough. Continue to roll dough until you have the shape of a strudel.

Bake on a sheet pan with wax paper at 350° for 20 minutes until golden brown.

Cooking Secret: You can prepare this strudel a day in advance. Make sure you cover it before refrigerating. Just pop it in the oven and you are ready to sit down to a delicious seafood dish.

Serves 6
Preparation Time:
  15 Minutes
Preheat oven to 350°

20 bay scallops
 1 lb. crab meat, jumbo
   lump
 8 large shrimps, cubed
 1 lb. cream cheese,
   softened
   White pepper to taste
 1 tsp. Old Bay Seasoning
 1 tsp. dill weed sprigs,
   chopped fine
   Juice from 1 lemon
 2 Tbsps. lobster base
 2 Tbsps. dry sherry wine
 4 phyllo dough sheets,
   14 × 18 inches

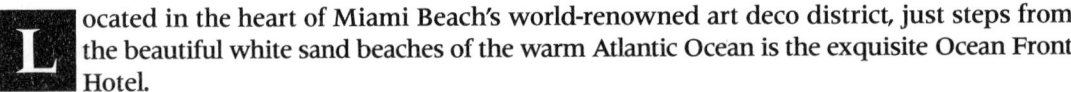

OCEAN FRONT HOTEL

1230-38 Ocean Drive
Miami Beach 33139
(800) 783-1725
(305) 672-2579
Room Rates: $135–$475

Located in the heart of Miami Beach's world-renowned art deco district, just steps from the beautiful white sand beaches of the warm Atlantic Ocean is the exquisite Ocean Front Hotel.

The hotel's rooms are delightfully decorated with a Mediterranean theme, complete with authentic furnishings from the 1930s. Each guest room offers a private in-room safe, color television, VCR, stereo with CD player, wet bar with refrigerator, soundproof windows, beach towels, bathrobes and central air conditioning. Many rooms have balconies with breathtaking ocean or courtyard views. For those choosing one of the penthouse suites, not only will you have wonderful ocean views from your private balcony, but the added bonus of a whirlpool tub and a private elevator.

While staying at the Ocean Front Hotel, be sure to sample some of the fine cuisine at the hotel's brasserie-style Les Deux Fontaines French Restaurant, which has a casual atmosphere and impeccable service.

Bouillabaisse

I n a large casserole, heat olive oil. Add all the vegetables, stirring, and let cook for a few minutes. Add Pastis and let reduce for 1 minute.

On top of the vegetables, place all the fish, cover with fish stock, add saffron and salt and pepper to taste. Slowly cook the bouillabaisse for 10 to 12 minutes or until the fish is done.

Serve in large soup plates with garlic croutons, rouille and Swiss cheese.

* Pastis, similar to Pernod, is a clear, strong, licorice-flavored apéritif that is very popular in southern France. It is usually mixed with water, which turns it whitish and cloudy.

Serves 6
Preparation Time:
  20 Minutes

  3 oz. olive oil
  1 large onion, diced
  4 large tomatoes, diced
  6 cloves garlic, crushed
  1 fennel bulb, sliced
  1 potato, thinly sliced
  1 leek, sliced
  1 oz. Pastis*
  3 lbs. assorted fresh local fish (e.g. red snapper, monkfish, black bass, shrimps or lobster), cut into pieces
  2 qts. fish stock
     Pinch of saffron
     Salt and black pepper to taste
     Garlic croutons for garnish
     Rouille for garnish
     Swiss cheese, grated for garnish

OMNI COLONNADE HOTEL

180 Aragon Avenue
Coral Gables, Florida 33134
(800) 533-1337
(305) 441-2600
Room Rates: $215–$445

In the heart of Coral Gables is a historic jewel featuring stunning architecture, exquisite furnishings and unsurpassed personal service. The Omni Colonnade Hotel surrounds you with a lavish array of amenities, from the complimentary champagne upon arrival to nightly turndown service.

Each of the 140 oversized deluxe guest rooms is elegantly appointed with marble baths and hand-tooled mahogany armoires. The hotel offers a fully-equipped exercise room, pool, whirlpool and sauna. Tennis, golf, boating, deep-sea fishing and other recreational activities are available as well.

Fufu Grouper with Papaya Guacamole

Boil the plantain with the skin on for approximately 1½ hours, until it is very soft. Remove from the water and discard the skin. Reserve the water.

Hand mash the plantain while adding ¼ cup of olive oil and the butter. If necessary add some of the reserved water to thin it out into a very thick but spreadable paste. Season with salt and pepper. Set the Fufu aside.

In a hot sauté pan, sear the grouper filets in 2 Tbsps. olive oil. Place fish in a baking dish and cover with the Fufu mixture.

Bake in 375° oven for 10 to 15 minutes, depending on the thickness of the fish.

For the guacamole: Combine the papaya, avocado, onion, garlic and lemon juice in a bowl and spoon the mixture next to the fish. Serve immediately.

Cooking Secret: Since the fish has a thick coating, the cooking time is increased by 30 to 40 percent over that for uncoated fish.

Serves 4
Preparation Time:
  2½ Hours
Preheat oven to 375°

  1 **large green plantain**
  ¼ **cup + 2 Tbsps. olive oil**
  ¼ **cup butter**
    Salt and pepper to taste
  4 **grouper filets, 6 to 8 oz. each**
  1 **ripe papaya, diced**
  1 **ripe avocado, diced**
  ¼ **cup Vidalia onion, finely diced**
  1 **Tbsp. garlic, minced**
  2 **Tbsps. fresh lemon juice**

☆

PELICAN HOTEL

826 Ocean Drive
Miami Beach, Florida 33139
(800) 7-PELICAN
(305) 673-3373
Web Site: www.pelicanhotel.com
E-mail: pelican@pelicanhotel.com
Room Rates: $125–$2,000

A wonderland of eclectic style, located on the ocean in the heart of South Beach, is the Pelican Hotel and Café. Owned by the Italian clothing conglomerate Diesel Jeans International, this Fellini-esque property is extremely quirky. The 25 custom-designed theme rooms and suites are decorated with original art deco vintage furnishings, and each has oak floors, air conditioning, refrigerator and VCR/CD sound system.

Visually striking, the Pelican Café, headed by Chef Andrea Comini, offers an interesting menu that is versatile and eclectic, from an afternoon snack right into an exquisite dinner. Menu highlights include Poppy Seed-Crusted Tuna Carpaccio, homemade fresh Mozzarella Rolled with Parma Prosciutto and Spinach, New Zealand Baby Lamb Chops, Pan Roasted Atlantic Salmon on Scallion Mashed Potatoes with Lemon and Thyme Sour Cream, followed by a Mango Crème Brûlé and Melting Chocolate Tart.

Guacamole Crostini

lace avocado, red bell pepper, red onion, lemon juice, Tabasco Sauce, salt and pepper in a large mixing bowl and mash together.

Slice bread into 4 slices.

Cut Brie cheese into thin slices. Place on top of bread slices. Place in a 450° oven for 1 minute or until the brie is slightly melted. Remove from the oven and spread avocado salsa on top of the cheese.

Garnish with sun-dried tomatoes.

Serves 4
Preparation Time:
 15 Minutes
Preheat oven to 450°

3 avocados, seeded,
  diced
1 red bell pepper,
  seeded, diced
$\frac{1}{3}$ red onion, diced
  Juice from 2 lemons
2 Tbsps. Tabasco Sauce
  Salt and pepper to
  taste
  Ciabatta bread or
  French baguette
3 oz. French Brie cheese
2 Tbsps. sun-dried
  tomatoes for garnish

Coconut Ceviche

Serves 2
Preparation Time:
15 Minutes
(note refrigeration time)

10 oz. yellowfin tuna, cut
    into ½-inch cubes
2 Tbsps. chives, chopped
¼ cup red onion,
    julienned
    Juice from 3 lemons
    Juice from 2 limes
4 cups coconut milk
1 coconut

lace tuna in a bowl. Refrigerate. Place chives in a separate bowl. Add the onion, citrus juices and coconut milk. Refrigerate.

Five minutes before serving, marinate the tuna in the bowl with the coconut-citrus mixture.

Cut the coconut in half to create bowls. Serve the tuna in the coconut bowls.

Rigatoni Bok Choy

Wash the bok choy and drain very well. Place on a cutting board. Remove the white stems and cut the greens thinly. Place the greens in a pan and sauté in extra virgin olive oil. Stir-fry for 2 to 3 minutes.

Add the prosciutto to the pan and continue cooking for 5 more minutes, stirring constantly. Add the cream and seasonings and let the sauce reduce for 8 minutes.

Cook the pasta according to directions. Drain the rigatoni and add it to the sauce. Stir to combine and sprinkle with Parmesan cheese before serving.

Serves 4
Preparation Time:
  15 Minutes

1 bunch bok choy
¼ cup extra virgin olive oil
3 oz. air-dried prosciutto
¼ cup heavy cream
  Salt and pepper to taste
1 lb. rigatoni pasta
¼ cup Parmesan cheese, grated

☆

New Zealand Baby Lamb Chops with Mashed Potatoes and Spinach in Balsamic Sauce

Serves 2
Preparation Time:
  25 Minutes
Preheat oven to 350°

32 oz. lamb rack
 1 sprig fresh rosemary,
   chopped
   Salt and pepper to
   taste
 5 medium potatoes
½ lb. spinach leaves,
   washed
½ cup vegetable oil
 3 Tbsps. unsalted butter
 1 cup warm milk
½ cup Italian balsamic
   vinegar

ut the lamb rack in a roasting pan. Sprinkle with rosemary, salt and pepper and bake at 350° for 25 minutes.

Bring 1 gallon of salted water to a boil. Peel the potatoes and cut in half. Add them to the salted, boiling water.

Soak spinach in cold water and drain.

Heat the vegetable oil in a sauté pan. Add the spinach and stir-fry for 2 minutes.

Drain the potatoes and mash with butter, milk and salt and pepper to taste. Set aside.

Using the same pan used for the lamb chops, add the vinegar and reduce by half.

Remove the rack of lamb from the oven and slice between the bones. Place 1 scoop of mashed potatoes in the center of each serving dish. Arrange the lamb chops around the potatoes. Pour the vinegar reduction over the lamb and place warm spinach on top of the lamb-chop bone.

☆

Warm Chocolate Cake
with Molten Liquid Center

Melt the chocolate in a bain-marie. Add the butter. In a bowl, mix together the flour and sugar. Then add it to the chocolate mixture.

Beat the eggs and yolks together. Add the vanilla extract, then incorporate the egg mixture into the chocolate mixture.

Pour the chocolate into two 2-inch aluminum cups. Bake in the oven at 350° for 7 minutes. Unmold, sprinkle with powdered sugar and serve with vanilla ice cream.

Serves 2
Preparation Time:
   15 Minutes
Preheat oven to 350°

   8 oz. semisweet
      chocolate
   8 Tbsps. (1 stick)
      unsalted butter,
      melted
   $\frac{1}{3}$ cup all-purpose flour
   $\frac{3}{4}$ cup granulated white
      sugar
   4 eggs
   2 egg yolks
   2 Tbsps. vanilla extract
   4 Tbsps. powdered sugar
1$\frac{1}{2}$ cups vanilla ice cream

REGISTRY RESORT

475 Seagate Drive
Naples, Florida 34103
(800) 247-9810
(941) 597-3232
Room Rates: $140–$305

The Registry Resort is the rarest of combinations—impeccable standards of luxury and the untamed splendor of Florida. From blue herons and roseate spoonbills to raccoons and otters, guests enjoy the most spectacular sights and sounds of Southwest Florida. At the end of the boardwalk lies a secluded beach of snow-white sand and crystal-clear water. Guests can spend the day swimming, snorkeling, shelling, sailing, wind-surfing or surf-fishing.

While all 395 guest rooms and 29 suites in the Registry's tower are conceived as luxurious homes away from home, each offers a very special feature that home is not likely to have: a breathtaking view overlooking the Gulf from a grand-sized balcony. There is nothing quite like gazing at the splendor of Florida's legendary sunsets.

From the casual to the sublime, dining and entertainment at the Registry are always a matter of good taste. Variety is abundant, with a selection of seven superb restaurants and lounges.

Macadamia Nut Banana-Crusted Orange Roughy with Citrus Vanilla Bean Sauce

F or the sauce: In a saucepan, put the lemon and lime juices and zests, white wine, shallots, peppercorns and bay leaf. Split the vanilla bean in half lengthwise and add to the pot. Simmer until almost all the liquid is reduced.

Add the cream and reduce by half, then remove from heat. Quickly whisk in the butter. Season to taste with salt and pepper.

Combine the banana chips and macadamia nuts. Set aside.

Season the orange roughy filets with salt and pepper. Dredge the filets in flour and shake off excess. Dip in the egg mixture. Place in the banana-nut mixture and coat well.

Sauté in oil on both sides over medium heat until lightly browned. Place in a 350° oven for 4 to 8 minutes or until the fish flakes.

Serves 6
Preparation Time:
 45 Minutes
Preheat oven to 350°

 Juice and zest from
 1 lemon
 Juice and zest from
 1 lime
 $1/2$ cup white wine
 2 shallots, chopped
 4 to 5 white peppercorns
 1 bay leaf
 $1/2$ vanilla bean
 $1/2$ cup heavy cream
 2 Tbsps. butter
 Salt and pepper to
 taste
 3 cups banana chips,
 dried, crumbled
 3 cups macadamia nuts,
 crumbled
 6 orange roughy filets,
 6 to 8 oz. each
 1 cup flour
 2 eggs, beaten with
 $1/2$ cup milk
 2 Tbsps. vegetable oil

☆

RITZ-CARLTON® NAPLES

280 Vanderbilt Beach Road
Naples, Florida 34108-2300
(800) 241-3333
(941) 598-3300
Web Site: www.ritzcarlton.com
Room Rates: $170–$3,500

T he resort is located on more than 19 beachfront acres, offering views of the Gulf of Mexico from the 463 guest rooms and suites. The hotel is decorated with British and American art from the 18th and 19th centuries, offset with marble and with crystal chandeliers. Guest rooms are appointed with armoires, writing desks, separate dressing areas with vanities and private balconies.

Three miles of pure white sand beach fronts the serene Gulf waters. Sailboats and catamarans are available, as well as chaise lounges with sun shades and menu beverage service. The pool, with a large deck area, tennis with six lighted courts and a fully staffed fitness center are here for your enjoyment. In addition, guests enjoy preferred golfing privileges at several area championship courses.

The Ritz-Carlton offers a choice of 8 restaurants, including the Dining Room, noted for its Floridian cuisine with Asian influences, and the award-winning Grill, a favorite for hearty classic cuisine with a fine selection of vintage wines.

Seared Snapper
in Yellow Tomato Vinaigrette

S eason the snapper filets with salt and pepper. Heat a non-stick pan. Add the clarified butter and sear the fish, skin side down first, for 3 minutes on each side. Remove the snapper filets from the pan.

To serve, spoon the vinaigrette around the snapper.

For the vinaigrette: Place the large tomatoes and vinegar in a blender and mix on the highest speed for 30 seconds. On slow speed, gradually add the olive oil until well blended. Season to taste with salt and pepper.

Halve the pear tomatoes and add to the vinaigrette. Add the shallots. Allow to stand at room temperature.

Serves 4
Preparation Time:
  15 Minutes

  4 snapper filets, skin on,
    7 oz. each
    Salt and pepper to
    taste
  1 cup clarified butter
    Yellow Tomato
    Vinaigrette (recipe
    follows)

Vinaigrette:

  4 large yellow tomatoes,
    blanched, skinned,
    seeded
  6 Tbsps. rice wine
    vinegar
  1 cup extra virgin olive
    oil
    Salt and pepper to
    taste
 16 yellow pear tomatoes
  6 shallots, finely diced

☆

ROYAL PALM HOUSE
BED AND BREAKFAST

3215 Spruce Avenue
West Palm Beach, Florida 33407
(800) 655-3196
(561) 863-9836
Room Rates: $75–$150

The Royal Palm House Bed and Breakfast was built in 1925, during the West Palm Beach land boom. This tropical Dutch Colonial-style home features single guest rooms and suites with private baths.

Each room has its own unique style of furnishing and atmosphere. The spacious grounds are planted with lush tropical vegetation, which surrounds the lovely freeform swimming pool. It is a great place to relax and sunbathe.

The West Palm Beach area is located on Florida's "Gold Coast," named for the gold salvaged from shipwrecks off the coast. Besides having some of the most beautiful beaches in the world, there are numerous theaters and playhouses, Worth Avenue for shopping, plus numerous golf courses, tennis courts, croquet clubs and polo fields here.

Low-Fat Italian-Style French Toast

Beat together the egg substitute, skim milk and orange juice. Soak bread in mixture.

Place in a non-stick baking pan. Place in 350° oven for about 20 minutes. Top with orange zest and powdered sugar.

Serve with low-calorie syrup.

Serves 2
Preparation Time:
 25 Minutes
Preheat oven to 350°

  1 cup egg substitute
 ¼ cup skim milk
 ¼ cup orange juice
  4 French or Italian bread
     slices, 3 inches thick
     Zest from ½ orange for
     garnish
     Powdered sugar for
     garnish

☆

Rotini with Calamari and Eggplant

Serves 4
Preparation Time:
 1 Hour 10 Minutes

 1 cup white wine
 2 Tbsps. garlic, chopped
 10 oz. tomatoes, chopped
 1 cup mushrooms,
  chopped
 1 medium eggplant,
  peeled, diced
 1 Tbsp. curry powder
 1 Tbsp. tarragon,
  crushed
  Salt and pepper to
  taste
 ½ lb. rotini pasta
 ½ lb. fresh baby calamari,
  cleaned

U sing a non-stick frying pan with a lid, boil the wine with the garlic. Add tomatoes, mushrooms, eggplant, curry powder, tarragon and salt and pepper. Lower heat and simmer, covered, for 1 hour.

Bring 5 qts. water to boil. When water is boiling and there is 8 minutes left to cook the sauce, add the pasta to the water and the calamari to the sauce.

When pasta is cooked al dente, drain, put it in a large serving bowl. Pour sauce over the pasta and mix.

Cooking Secret: Serve with a nice, full-bodied red wine.

★

Chicken Breast with Balsamic Vinegar

I n a non-stick frying pan with a lid, boil the balsamic vinegar with the garlic. Add the chicken breasts and sprinkle over it 1 tsp. sage. Cover and cook for 5 minutes.

Turn the breasts and sprinkle with the remaining sage, salt and pepper. Cover loosely and lower heat to simmer. Cook until vinegar begins to thicken, about 40 minutes.

Serve and pour remaining juices over chicken.

Cooking Secret: A nice, fruity white wine is great with this chicken.

Serves 4
Preparation Time:
   50 Minutes

¾ cup balsamic vinegar
4 Tbsps. garlic, chopped
4 chicken breasts
2 tsps. sage
   Salt and pepper to
   taste

☆

SANIBEL HARBOUR RESORT AND SPA

17260 Harbour Pointe Drive
Fort Myers, Florida 33908
(800) 767-7777
(941) 466-4000
Web Site: www.sanibel-resort.com
Room Rates: $120–$525

S anibel Harbour Resort and Spa is a secluded luxury hotel on San Carlos Bay. Situated on a private peninsula overlooking Florida's southwest coast with spectacular vistas and breathtaking sunsets, this modern hotel evokes a turn-of-the-century feeling with its cupola-topped pavilion.

Amid 80 acres of unspoiled natural beauty, the 319-room resort offers guests world-class facilities, including a European spa and fitness center, championship tennis courts and fine dining. All the guest rooms have private balconies and spectacular views of the Sanibel and Captiva Islands.

Mushroom Ravioli
with Light Tomato Concassé

I n a large saucepan, heat the olive oil over low heat. Add the mushrooms, garlic and thyme and sauté for 5 minutes. Set aside to cool.

Place 20 wonton wrappers flat on the table. Brush with egg wash. Place mushroom mixture in the center of each square. Cover each with another wrapper, making sure the edges of the wrappers are pressed together. Use more egg wash if needed to seal. Refrigerate while you prepare the concassé.

In a medium saucepan, heat the olive oil. Add the onions and tomatoes and sauté for 5 minutes. Add the white wine and cook for 10 more minutes. Keep warm until time to serve.

When ready to serve ravioli, bring 3 qts. water and 1 Tbsp. olive oil to a boil. Lower heat and poach ravioli for 5 minutes. Drain.

To serve, ladle ½ cup tomato concassé on each of the four plates and surround with 5 ravioli. Garnish with basil leaves.

Cooking Secret: This appetizer has only 100 calories and 3 grams of fat per serving. Delicious and healthy!

Serves 4
Preparation Time:
 25 Minutes

- 1 tsp. olive oil
- 1 cup shiitake mushrooms or morels, chopped
- 1 clove garlic, chopped
- 1 Tbsp. fresh thyme, chopped
- 40 wonton wrappers
- 1 egg, beaten with 1 tsp. water
- 1 Tbsp. olive oil
  Fresh basil leaves for garnish

Concassé:
Yield: 2 cups

- 1 tsp. olive oil
- ¼ cup onions, diced
- 4 tomatoes, peeled, chopped
- 1 cup dry white wine

Couscous Tabbouleh

Serves 4
Preparation Time:
  15 Minutes
(note refrigeration time)

  4 cups wheat couscous,
     cooked
  4 bunches parsley,
     chopped fine
  4 tomatoes, diced
  1 bunch scallions,
     chopped
  2 bunches mint,
     chopped
     Juice from 5 lemons
  3 Tbsps. extra virgin
     olive oil
     Pepper to taste

Place couscous in a bowl. Add the tomatoes, parsley, mint and scallions and mix together. Add the lemon juice and olive oil. Season to taste.

Refrigerate for 30 to 40 minutes to allow couscous to absorb liquid.

Floridian Orange Light Cheesecake

S train the yogurt through cheesecloth to make yogurt cheese. Pour yogurt into cheesecloth and tie ends of the cheesecloth together. Put in a colander over a plate and refrigerate for 6 to 8 hours.

Cook the juice of the orange and the zests over medium heat, reducing to ¼ cup. Set aside.

In a large mixing bowl, combine the sour cream, sugar substitute, yogurt cheese, flour, honey and juice-zest reduction.

In a medium bowl, whip the egg whites until firm, like meringue. Gradually fold egg yolks into egg whites.

Add the egg mixture to the yogurt mixture in the large mixing bowl and mix evenly.

In a small mixing bowl, mix graham cracker crumbs, cinnamon, vanilla extract and margarine together.

Press the crust mixture into a pie pan. Pour the yogurt mixture into the crust and bake for 20 to 25 minutes or until center is firm.

Serves 10
Preparation Time:
 45 Minutes
(note refrigeration time)
Preheat oven to 325°

 2 cups nonfat plain
   yogurt
 1 cup orange juice
   Zest from 1 orange
   Zest from 1 lemon
 ½ cup nonfat sour cream
 6 packets sugar
   substitute, such as
   Equal or Sweet 'n Low
 4 Tbsps. all-purpose
   flour
 2 Tbsps. honey
 2 egg whites
 2 egg yolks

Crust:

1½ cups graham cracker
   crumbs
 1 tsp. ground cinnamon
 2 tsps. vanilla extract
 8 Tbsps. (1 stick) low-fat
   margarine

ANTONIO'S LA FIAMMA

ITALIAN CUISINE
611 South Orlando Avenue
Maitland, Florida
(407) 645-5523
Lunch Monday–Friday 11:30AM–2:30PM
Dinner Monday–Thursday 5PM–10PM
Dinner Friday and Saturday 5PM–11PM
Average Dinner For Two: $55

One of the restaurants favored by locals in Central Florida, Antonio's La Fiamma is well known for its friendly, professional service and Northern Italian cuisine. The open kitchen showcases the chef's display of artful dishes while filling the restaurant with tantalizing aromas.

Among mouth-watering appetizers are the fresh portobello mushrooms marinated in lemon juice, a touch of balsamic vinegar, olive oil and fresh rosemary, then grilled over an open wood fire. The antipasto assortment features fresh mozzarella, Italian cured meats and an assortment from the daily antipasto table.

Pastas of the house include penne pasta with chunks of fresh salmon, cream, vodka and a touch of tomato. The homemade raviolis are stuffed with shiitake mushrooms in a pink sauce with fresh tomatoes, mushrooms and a touch of cream.

Entrée highlights are veal chops sautéed with fresh herbs, cognac and lemon, chicken breasts filled with roasted peppers, cheese, spinach and prosciutto and eggplant dipped in light batter and filled with cheese and sun-dried tomatoes before being baked in a wood-burning stove.

Save room for dessert. Tempting choices include Italian lemon shells filled with imported Italian sorbet, homemade cheesecakes and Belgian chocolate cups filled with brandy cream and surrounded by fresh raspberry sauce.

ANTONIO'S LA FIAMMA'S MENU FOR TWO:

Fish Soup

Penne alla Vodka

Veal Chops alla Senese

Fish Soup

I n a sauté pan, warm 1 Tbsp. olive oil over medium-high heat.
Add the bay leaves, garlic and parsley. Let cook 2 minutes or until the garlic becomes golden.

Add the fish, crab meat, mussels, clams and ½ cup wine. Reduce heat and stir frequently, cooking for about 3 minutes.

Add the fish stock and tomato sauce and simmer for 10 minutes. Season with salt and pepper to taste.

Add the shrimp to the sauce, cooking for about 3 minutes or until shrimp is cooked through.

In a separate sauté pan, warm 1 Tbsp. olive oil. Pour approximately ¾ cup of the liquid from the first saucepan into the second.

Add the linguine to warm up over medium-high heat, stirring often. Cook 3 minutes while mixing.

Add the remaining ½ cup of wine to the seafood pan. Let cook, stirring, for 3 minutes. Pour the seafood over the linguine. Let simmer over low heat for 3 minutes.

Serve in large pasta bowls.

Serves 2
Preparation Time:
  25 Minutes

  2 Tbsps. olive oil
  3 bay leaves
  2 Tbsps. garlic, chopped
    fine
  2 Tbsps. parsley,
    chopped fine
  ⅓ lb. cod filet or other
    firm white fish, cut
    into 2-inch chunks
  ⅓ lb. fresh crab meat
  4 black mussels
  6 baby clams
  1 cup dry white wine
  1 cup fish stock
  1½ cups fresh tomato
    sauce
    Salt and black pepper
    to taste
  4 large shrimp
  1 cup linguine pasta,
    cooked

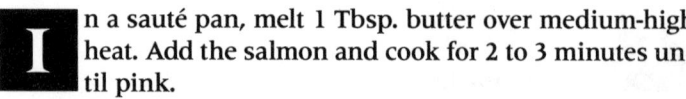

Penne alla Vodka

Serves 2
Preparation Time:
  20 Minutes

  2 **Tbsps. unsweetened**
    butter
  6 **oz. Norwegian smoked**
    or fresh salmon, finely
    chopped
  ¾ **cup tomato sauce**
    Salt and black pepper
    to taste
  ½ **cup whipping cream**
  1½ **cups penne pasta,**
    cooked
  2 **oz. 80-proof vodka**
  1 **Tbsp. fresh parsley,**
    finely chopped

In a sauté pan, melt 1 Tbsp. butter over medium-high heat. Add the salmon and cook for 2 to 3 minutes until pink.

Slowly add the tomato sauce, then salt and pepper to taste. Stirring frequently, let sauce cook for 2 minutes over medium heat.

Reduce heat and add the cream, cooking until the sauce thickens, about 3 to 4 minutes.

Place the cooked pasta in hot tap water for a few seconds and drain well. Drop the pasta into the sauce over medium heat. Heat the pasta for 2 minutes, stirring constantly.

Add the vodka and the remaining 1 Tbsp. butter. Salt and pepper to taste. Stir over low heat until the sauce is creamy, about 3 to 4 minutes.

Garnish with fresh parsley before serving.

☆

Veal Chops alla Senese

Slice the veal chops horizontally, ¾ of the way to the bone. Stuff the chops with prosciutto.

In a shallow bowl beat the egg with the salt. Coat the veal chop thoroughly with the egg mixture, then dip into the bread crumbs.

In a sauté pan, warm the butter, olive oil and the sprig of rosemary over medium-high heat. Remove the rosemary after 2 minutes.

Sear both sides of the chop in the oil-butter mixture for 3 to 4 minutes over medium-high heat. Lower the heat to medium.

Remove the chops from the sauté pan and place in a roasting pan. Add the brandy and wine. Bake in a 350° oven for 8 to 10 minutes. Add a little more wine if the chops gets too dry.

Squeeze lemon over the veal chops before serving.

Cooking Secret: This dish is excellent with roasted potatoes.

Serves 2
Preparation Time:
  20 Minutes
Preheat oven to 350°

- 2 **veal chops on the bone, 12 oz. each, trimmed of fat**
- 2 **slices prosciutto di Parma**
- 1 **egg**
- ¼ **tsp. salt**
- 1 **cup fine bread crumbs**
- 2 **Tbsps. unsalted butter**
- 2 **Tbsps. olive oil**
- 1 **fresh rosemary sprig**
- 1 **oz. brandy**
- ¼ **cup Chardonnay**
- 1 **lemon**

BIJOU CAFÉ

CONTINENTAL CUISINE
1287 First Street
Sarasota, Florida 34236
(941) 366-8111
Lunch Monday–Friday 11:30AM–2:30PM
Dinner Nightly 5PM–11PM
Average Dinner For Two: $65

V oted one of the Best Continental, Most Romantic and Most Popular restaurants in the country by Zagat Survey, it is easy to see why reservations are a must at Bijou Café. This stylish bistro is the epitome of European sophistication and charm. The restaurant's exterior is sparkling white with hunter green awnings and trim. The interior walls are peach with dark green pillars, chair rail moldings and brass-and-glass candle wall sconces. The tables are covered by white tablecloths, with flickering white candles and a single perfect orchid on each.

Owner and chef Jean-Pierre Knaggs bought the restaurant in 1986. Built in the 1930s, the site was originally a Texaco service station. Initially Chef Jean-Pierre focused on traditional Continental cuisine. Due to his travels abroad and his own South African upbringing (by a French mother), it was only natural for him to take Continental cuisine further.

The restaurant's signature dish is its *Pommes Gratin Dauphinoise*—sliced potatoes covered with cream, garlic and Gruyère cheese and baked. Chef Jean-Pierre learned the secret of this incredible dish at the L'Oustreau de Beaumanière, a world-class hotel and restaurant in les Baux de Provence. Other equally sinful dishes include Spicy Hot Shrimp Piri-Piri Sautéed with Garlic, Lemon and Cayenne, Veal Louisville with Pecans, Pears and Kentucky-Bourbon Sauce, Handmade Ravioli Stuffed with Two Cheeses and Spinach, Served with Creamy Tomato Basil Sauce and a Totally Awesome Chocolate Madness.

BIJOU CAFÉ'S MENU FOR FOUR:

Chilled Curried Carrot and Apple Soup

Grilled Marinated Vegetable and Pasta Salad

Leg of Lamb in Puff Pastry

Warm Sauté of Summer Fruit

Totally Awesome Chocolate Madness

Chilled Curried Carrot and Apple Soup

I n a saucepan, sauté the onion in butter until soft and translucent. Add the curry powder and flour, and, while stirring, sauté a few minutes longer to cook the flour. Now add the rest of the ingredients and simmer for 20 minutes or until the carrots are very soft and well cooked.

Purée the soup in a food processor, using the pulse method. The soup is more interesting if there is some texture to it, so don't purée it totally smooth. Chill for at least 8 hours.

Serve in chilled bowls and garnish with a dollop of whipped cream or sour cream, a few slivers of apple and a dusting of curry powder.

Serves 4
Preparation Time:
 20 Minutes
(note chilling time)

½ cup onion, chopped
 1 Tbsp. butter
 1 Tbsp. curry powder
 1 Tbsp. flour
 1 cup carrots, chopped
 2 medium Granny
   Smith apples, peeled,
   cored, chopped,
   reserve a few slices for
   garnish
½ tsp. cumin
 2 tsps. apple cider
   vinegar
 3 cups chicken stock
   Salt and white pepper
   to taste
½ cup whipped cream or
   sour cream for garnish
   Curry powder for
   dusting

Grilled Marinated Vegetable and Pasta Salad

Serves 4
Preparation Time:
  40 Minutes
Preheat oven to 375°

  1 head of garlic
    Olive oil
  1 small zucchini
  1 red pepper
  1 red onion
  ½ small eggplant
  ¼ cup olive oil
  1 Tbsp. Dijon mustard
  2 Tbsps. balsamic
    vinegar
  2 tsps. herbes de
    Provence*
    Salt and pepper to
    taste
  2 cups cooked pasta,
    preferably shells or
    rotini

For the roasted garlic: Cut pointed end off garlic head, about ½-inch from the top, with a very sharp knife. Rub entire head with olive oil and place on an oven-proof dish in 375° oven. Bake about 30 minutes or until head is very soft and mushy. Set aside to cool.

Preheat coals or gas-fired grill. Slice all the vegetables into long, thin pieces. Place in a bowl and drizzle a little olive oil over them, turning to coat evenly. Grill quickly over moderate heat, just until they have grill marks and are limp.

Chop vegetables into ½-inch pieces. Set aside to cool while making the dressing.

Place mustard, vinegar and herbs in a deep salad bowl. Squeeze garlic head into mixture and start whisking with a wire whip. Slowly drizzle the rest of the olive oil into the mixture, while continuing to whisk. Dressing will thicken as it begins to emulsify. If it becomes too thick, add a little white wine or lemon juice. Season to taste with salt and pepper and then toss with all the vegetables and the pasta. Refrigerate until ready to serve.

* Herbes de Provence is an assortment of dried herbs said to reflect those most commonly used in southern France. The blend can be found packed in tiny clay crocks in the spice section of large supermarkets. The mixture commonly contains basil, fennel seed, lavender, marjoram, rosemary, sage, summer savory and thyme. The blend can be used to season dishes of meat, poultry and vegetables.

☆

Leg of Lamb in Puff Pastry

Sauté the mushrooms, shallots and garlic in the butter until soft. Deglaze with Madeira and add herbs and seasonings and cook until moisture is reduced.

Season inside of lamb with salt and pepper. Mix mushroom mixture with pâté and mustard and smear mixture inside lamb. Close and tie with several string loops.

Brown lamb in a large heated skillet or place in a 475° oven for 15 minutes.

Remove from oven, let cool and then wrap with thinly rolled puff pastry. Brush with egg yolk and return to oven for 20 more minutes for medium rare, 30 minutes for well done.

Serves 4 to 6
Preparation Time:
  45 Minutes
(note cooling time)

  5 oz. mushrooms, cut
     into quarters
  2 shallots, chopped
  3 cloves garlic, crushed
  2 Tbsps. butter
  4 oz. Madeira
  ½ tsp. each: thyme,
     rosemary and tarragon
     Salt and pepper to
     taste
  1 leg of lamb, boned
  4 oz. pâté (optional)
  2 Tbsps. Dijon mustard
     Oil
 12 oz. puff pastry
  1 egg yolk, beaten

☆

Warm Sauté of Summer Fruit

Serves 4
Preparation Time:
  15 Minutes

1½ Tbsps. unsalted butter
    or margarine
1½ Tbsps. sugar
  1 Tbsp. honey
  1 vanilla bean pod
  1 cup strawberries or
    pitted Bing cherries,
    sliced
  ¾ cup blueberries
  1 cup peaches,
    nectarines or peeled
    kiwi, sliced
  2 Tbsps. kirsch or to
    taste

Melt butter in a sauté pan or large skillet. Stir in sugar and honey. Split vanilla bean and scrape insides into the pan. Add the bean pod. Add fresh fruits and liqueur to taste. Cook over medium heat, basting with sauce, until fruits are warmed through. Do not overcook. Remove the bean pod before serving.

Cooking Secret: Use any combination of fresh fruit that looks beautiful together: grapes, cherries, berries, peaches, plums, nectarines, bananas. For a low-calorie dessert, serve as is, or serve with crème fraîche or whipped cream.

Totally Awesome Chocolate Madness

L ine a medium-sized stainless steel bowl or ovenproof bowl with aluminum foil. Combine chocolate, coffee and sugar in a saucepan and cook over medium heat, stirring all the time. When sugar has dissolved and chocolate is melted and smooth, place mixture in a mixing bowl. While beating at medium speed, add the butter in small amounts, waiting for each amount to be incorporated into the mixture before adding more. Then add the eggs, one at a time, using the same method. Add the vanilla and the Triple Sec and pour mixture into the prepared bowl.

Bake for about 35 minutes or until it is slightly puffed up around the edges. Let cool, then press edges down gently, cover with plastic wrap and refrigerate at least eight hours before serving.

Invert the chocolate cake onto a platter, garnish with whipped cream and fresh berries, and serve.

Serves 6 to 8
Preparation Time:
 1 Hour
(note refrigeration time)
Preheat oven to 350°

 8 oz. unsweetened
   baking chocolate
 ½ cup strong coffee
 1 cup sugar
 ½ lb. butter, softened
 4 eggs
   Dash of vanilla extract
   Dash of Triple Sec
   Whipped cream for
   garnish
   Fresh berries for
   garnish

☆

CAFÉ CREOLE AND OYSTER BAR

CAJUN AND CREOLE CUISINE
1330 East Ninth Avenue
Ybor City, Florida 33605
(813) 247-6283
Lunch and Dinner Monday–Thursday 11:30AM–10PM
Lunch and Dinner Friday & Saturday 11:30AM–11PM
Lunch Sunday Noon–4PM
Average Dinner for Two: $45

If you want to experience New Orleans in Florida, Café Creole and Oyster Bar is the place to go. Located in the historic El Pasaje building, the restaurant captures the spirit and excitement of bygone eras. Café Creole is a focal point for Tampa's night life and fine dining. Diners can feast in the landscaped outdoor courtyard and be serenaded by the water fountain, soaking up the sounds from the street. Each dish is made from scratch, using many local ingredients—some are even grown in the courtyard!

Some of the best items to try include Jambalaya, Oysters Rockefeller, Crawfish Etouffée, Blackened Shrimp, Fried Grouper and Praline Cheesecake.

CAFÉ CREOLE AND OYSTER BAR'S MENU FOR SIX:

Bar-B-Que Shrimp Orleans

Seafood Gumbo

Salad with Creole Mustard Vinaigrette

Louisiana Crab Cakes with Dill Sauce

Bread Pudding with Warm Whiskey Brandy Sauce

Bar-B-Que Shrimp Orleans

For the butter: Butter should be brought to room temperature. In a mixing bowl, whip all ingredients into the softened butter until evenly blended. Set aside in refrigerator. Can be kept refrigerated for a few weeks.

For the shrimp: Melt butter in a large sauté pan over medium-high heat. Add garlic and sauté for 1 minute; do not brown. Add shrimp and blackening spice and cook just until shrimp turn opaque. Add white wine and reduce by 2/3.

Remove pan from heat to keep herbal garlic butter from breaking, and immediately stir in the prepared seasoned butter until melted and creamy. You may need to return pan to heat briefly to melt the butter, but don't overheat as it will cause butter to separate.

Serve immediately with crusty French bread for butter sauce. Garnish with fresh chopped parsley.

Cooking Secret: Use shrimp heads and shells to make a great stock for gumbo.

Serves 6
Preparation Time:
  20 Minutes

Bar-B-Que Butter:

  ½ lb. butter
  1 Tbsp. garlic, chopped
  2 tsps. fish or seafood
    blackening spice
  2 tsps. Worcestershire
    sauce
  2 tsps. fresh lemon juice
  ½ tsp. black pepper
  ½ tsp. white pepper
  ½ tsp. whole leaf oregano
  ½ tsp. whole leaf thyme
  1 tsp. rosemary
  ½ tsp. salt

Shrimp:

  4 Tbsps. butter
  1 Tbsp. garlic, chopped
  24 large shrimps, peeled,
    deveined
  1 Tbsp. blackening spice
  4 Tbsps. white wine
  2 Tbsps. parsley,
    chopped for garnish

Seafood Gumbo

Serves 6
Preparation Time:
 30 Minutes

  3 Tbsps. corn or peanut
    oil
  3 Tbsps. all-purpose
    flour
  1 pint shrimp stock or
    clam juice (bottled)
    or plain water
  ¼ cup corn oil or peanut
    oil
  ½ lb. okra, cut into
    ¼-inch rounds
  ¾ cup bell pepper,
    chopped
  ½ cup celery, chopped
 1½ cups onion, chopped
 1½ Tbsps. garlic, chopped
    fine
  1 cup crushed tomatoes
    or tomato purée
  ½ tsp. whole leaf thyme
  3 bay leaves
 1½ tsps. fish or seafood
    blackening seasoning
 1½ tsps. salt
  ½ lb. small or medium
    shrimp, peeled,
    deveined, saving shells
    for stock
  ½ lb. blue crab meat
    (claw, special or lump)
  2 Tbsps. scallions,
    chopped fine
  4 Tbsps. fresh parsley,
    chopped fine

To make the roux, heat oil in frying pan until it smokes. Add flour, rapidly and continuously whisking it into oil until a peanut-butter color is reached. Set aside and keep warm to add to gumbo.

To make shrimp stock, bring shrimp shells and heads (if available) to a boil in a pint of water. Simmer for 15 minutes. Strain and set stock aside.

In large sauté pan, heat oil until very hot. Add okra and fry, stirring often. Cook until okra begins to brown, to cook away most of the slime.

Add bell pepper, celery, onion and garlic, continuing to stir often until vegetables begin to brown. Continue to stir and brown to begin to caramelize onion and other vegetables to create a rich, deep flavor in the gumbo.

Add tomatoes, stirring well, and cook for 5 minutes. Add thyme, bay leaves, blackening spice and salt and blend and cook for 2 more minutes. Add shrimp stock and bring to a boil.

Gradually and thoroughly whisk in still-warm roux, making sure to leave no lumps of roux in gumbo. With gumbo at a boil, add shrimp and cook for 2 minutes. Add crab meat and fold in gently so as not to shred. Add scallions and part of the parsley. Cook for 3 more minutes. Taste and adjust seasonings. For a spicier gumbo, add more blackening spice or cayenne pepper.

Serve in small bowls over about ¼ cup of warm white rice. Garnish top with the rest of the chopped fresh parsley.

Salad with Creole Mustard Vinaigrette

Wash and dry the salad greens and break into bite-sized pieces. Mix together and place in a large salad bowl. Place tomato wedges and cucumber slices around edge of bowl. Separate thin slices of Bermuda onion and cover center of salad bowl.

Put anchovy filets in a food processor or blender with garlic. Add lemon juice and red wine vinegar and purée. Add all other ingredients except olive oil and blend well. With machine in motion, slowly add olive oil to form a creamy, emulsified consistency.

Pour desired amount of dressing over greens.

Serves 6
Preparation Time:
  10 Minutes

  ⅓ head of Romaine
  1 head of Boston or Bibb lettuce
  ⅓ head of escarole
  2 ripe tomatoes, cut into 12 wedges
  1 cucumber, sliced into 24 slices
  1 Bermuda onion, sliced into 12 slices

Creole Mustard Vinaigrette:
Preparation Time:
  10 Minutes

  3 anchovy filets
  1 Tbsp. garlic, chopped fine
  2 Tbsps. fresh lemon juice
  3 Tbsps. red wine vinegar
  1 tsp. Dijon mustard
  2 tsps. dry whole leaf oregano
  ½ tsp. black pepper
  1 egg
  1 Tbsp. Creole mustard or stone-ground mustard
  1 tsp. Worcestershire sauce
  1½ tsps. Louisiana hot sauce
  1 cup extra virgin olive oil

★

Louisiana Crab Cakes with Dill Sauce

Serves 6 (12 Crab Cakes)
Preparation Time:
20 Minutes

1 egg
¼ cup milk
1½ cups stale French
  bread, diced into
  ½-inch cubes
½ lb. small shrimp
¼ cup butter
1 cup bell pepper,
  chopped fine
1½ cups onion, chopped
  fine
2 Tbsps. garlic, chopped
  fine
1 lb. blue crab meat
  (claw, special or lump)
1 to 2 tsps. fish or sea-
  food blackening spice
1 tsp. salt
⅓ cup Romano cheese,
  grated
½ cup fresh parsley,
  chopped fine
1½ cups bread crumbs
2 Tbsps. + 1 tsp. butter
¼ cup olive oil

Beat egg in a small bowl; add milk and blend well. Add diced bread cubes to soften and soak up the liquid. Set aside.

Chop shrimp into ½-inch pieces and set aside.

Melt butter in a 12-inch skillet and fry bell pepper, onion and garlic until brown, stirring often to get an even, brown, caramelized flavor. Add chopped shrimp and cook just until shrimp turn opaque, then turn off heat. Pick through crab meat for any shells and add crab to a mixing bowl with cooked shrimp and vegetables. Add soaked bread with egg and milk, seasonings, cheese and parsley and blend well but gently so as to leave crab meat in nice pieces. When ingredients are well blended, taste and add salt or extra blackening spice to taste. Form this mixture into 12 round crab cakes and lightly coat with plain fine bread crumbs.

Heat ⅓ stick of butter and olive oil in a large sauté pan and fry crab cakes until golden brown. Can be kept warm on a platter in oven. Serve with a dollop of dill sauce and a wedge of lemon.

Dill Sauce
Preparation Time: 10 Minutes
(note refrigeration time)

1 cup sour cream
½ cup mayonnaise
2 oz. fresh lemon juice
4 Tbsps. dill pickle relish
2 Tbsps. onion, chopped very fine
2 Tbsps. fresh dill or 1 Tbsp. dry dill, chopped fine
½ tsp. white pepper

Blend all ingredients well in a mixing bowl and refrigerate.

Bread Pudding
with Warm Whiskey Brandy Sauce

Beat eggs well and put in a mixing bowl with milk, cream and bread cubes. Mix until bread soaks up liquid well and is very soft. Add all other ingredients and mix well. Pour mixture into a 9 by 9-inch glass or metal baking pan. Place in a large metal baking pan with ½ inch of water in it and bake at 350° for one hour.

Cut into 6 equal squares and serve warm with warm Whiskey Brandy Sauce.

For the sauce: In a saucepan melt butter and mix in brown sugar until dissolved. Add all other ingredients, blend well and simmer over low heat. Cook for 10 minutes, stirring often.

Serve over warm Bread Pudding.

Serves 6
Preparation Time:
　20 to 30 Minutes
Preheat oven to 350°

　4 **large eggs**
　2 **cups milk**
　¾ **cup heavy cream**
　5 **cups stale French**
　　bread, cut into 1-inch
　　cubes
　2 **tsps. vanilla extract**
　½ **cup sugar**
　½ **cup raisins**
　¼ **cup pineapple, crushed**
　¼ **cup pecans, chopped**
　1 **tsp. cinnamon**

Whiskey Brandy Sauce:

　6 **Tbsps. butter**
　1 **cup light brown sugar**
　¼ **cup heavy cream**
　½ **cup half and half**
　1½ **tsps. whiskey or**
　　bourbon
　1½ **tsps. brandy**

☆

CAFÉ TU TU TANGO

ECLECTIC "APPETIZER" CUISINE
8625 International Drive
Orlando, Florida 32819
(407) 248-2222
Web Site: www.cafetututango.com
Open Monday–Thursday 11:30AM–11PM
Open Friday and Saturday 11:30AM–1AM
Average Dinner for Two: $40

T his fun and lively Bohemian hot spot in Orlando resembles a wild artist's loft in Barcelona, Spain. There is always a party going on. Local artists paint and display their work throughout this amusing restaurant. It is customary for a diner to sit down to dinner and see an artist staring at a blank canvas. By dessert, the artist is signing his or her name to their latest masterpiece.

The menu is an all-appetizer extravaganza incorporating the flavors of Spain, Italy, Latin American, Asia, the Caribbean and the Middle East with several notable highlights, including Cajun Chicken Egg Rolls made with diced blackened chicken, fresh corn, red onions, cheddar and goat cheeses, served on a bed of salsa roja with a side of Creole mustard dipping sauce. Jim Beam BBQ Wings and Ribs are grilled and served with a nest of Crispy Onions. Crazy Bananas are scoops of Banana Walnut Gelato topped with homemade Caramel Sauce flavored with Scotch and Drambuie. Scrumptious.

CAFÉ TU TU TANGO MENU FOR SIX:

Cajun Chicken Egg Rolls

Barcelona Stir-Fry

Guava Cheesecake

Cajun Chicken Egg Rolls

Mix Cajun seasoning and 1 cup vegetable oil to make marinade. Dip chicken breasts in marinade, then lightly brown on both sides in a hot skillet. Remove the chicken from the skillet and place in a 400° oven for 10 minutes or until cooked through. Remove, cool and cut into ¼-inch strips.

In a bowl, combine the chicken, corn, red onion, cilantro and cheeses and set aside.

In a separate bowl, mix the egg and milk to make an egg wash. Place a fully opened egg roll wrapper on a floured surface and brush with the egg wash. Place a tablespoon of filling on the egg roll wrapper, then fold diagonally into a cylinder shape.

Quickly fry the egg rolls in oil heated to 350° until golden brown.

Serve egg rolls with salsa roja and Creole mustard on the side.

Serves 6
Preparation Time:
  45 Minutes
Preheat oven to 400°

- ¼ cup Cajun blackening seasoning
- 1 cup vegetable oil
- 6 boneless chicken breasts, trimmed of excess fat
- 1 lb. whole-kernel corn, chopped
- ½ lb. red onion, diced
- 1 bunch cilantro, chopped
- 1 lb. cheddar cheese, shredded
- 2 oz. goat cheese
- 1 egg
- ½ cup milk
- 12 egg roll wrappers
  Vegetable oil for frying
- 1 jar salsa roja
- 1 jar Creole mustard

☆

Barcelona Stir-Fry

Serves 6
Preparation Time:
 45 Minutes

  2 boneless chicken
    breasts, cut into 1-inch
    pieces
  1 lb. calamari, cut into
    thin rings
  1 lb. small shrimp,
    peeled
  1 lb. andouille sausage,
    cut into 1-inch pieces
 ¼ cup olive oil
 ½ red pepper, thinly
    sliced
 ½ green pepper, thinly
    sliced
 ½ yellow pepper, thinly
    sliced
  2 lbs. button
    mushrooms, cut into
    fourths
  1 clove garlic, chopped
    Salt and pepper to
    taste
  1 pt. chicken stock
  1 cup white wine
  1 cup lemon juice
  6 cups rice, cooked

Cook the chicken, calamari, shrimp and andouille sausage in a heated skillet with ¼ cup oil for 3 minutes. Add the peppers, mushrooms, garlic, salt and pepper to the skillet.

In a separate bowl, combine the chicken stock, white wine and lemon juice and pour over the stir-fry. Cook until the broth has almost evaporated and the chicken and sausage are cooked through.

Serve over a bed of rice.

Guava Cheesecake

For the crust: Melt butter in a small saucepan. Stir in graham cracker crumbs. Grease an 8-inch springform pan and press graham cracker mixture into bottom. Chill.

For the filling: Beat cream cheese, sour cream, sugar, flour, egg yolks and egg whites together in a large mixing bowl. Stir in the vanilla extract, guava marmalade and orange peel. Beat until smooth.

Spoon the filling into the prepared crust.

Bake the cheesecake in a 400° oven for 15 minutes, then reduce temperature to 275° and bake 50 minutes more, or until the center of the cheesecake is firm to the touch. Cool before removing from the pan.

Garnish by spreading the remaining guava marmalade evenly on top.

Serves 6 to 8
Preparation Time:
1¼ Hours
(note refrigeration time)
Preheat oven to 400°

Crust:

¾ cup butter (1½ sticks)
1¾ cups graham cracker crumbs

Filling:

3 (8 oz.) packages cream cheese, softened
1 cup sour cream
⅔ cup sugar
2 Tbsps. all-purpose flour
5 egg yolks
3 egg whites
½ tsp. vanilla extract
10 oz. guava marmalade + 3 Tbsps. for garnish
Peel of 1 orange, finely grated

☆

FULTON'S CRAB HOUSE

SEAFOOD CUISINE
Pleasure Island
1670 Buena Vista Drive
Lake Buena Vista, Florida 32802
(407) 934-2628
Daily 11:30AM–2AM
Average Dinner For Two: $100

The concept for Fulton's Crab House is simple: good food in a high-energy atmosphere. This replica turn-of-the-century riverboat is a showplace filled with authentic artifacts and folk art describing the history of the sea. The dark colors of black and burgundy are accented with highly polished wood and brass details, with each deck having an individual character.

The seafood is delivered from local fishermen, international suppliers and other seafood connections to ensure only the freshest is served. The menu changes daily, reflecting the changing of the seasons. The chefs are constantly working with fresh ingredients to produce signature preparations and recipes.

Past house specialties have included Rock Shrimp Pasta with Roasted Peppers, Onions, Mushrooms and Tasso, Cioppino with Clams, Mussels, Crab, Shrimp, Scallops and Fresh Fish in Tomato Herb Broth, Charcoal Grilled Shrimp with Tomato, Basil and Garlic Chips over Rice, Sweet Scallops topped with Garlic Cheese Bread Crumbs, and Southeast Alaskan Halibut simmered in Smoked Tomato Broth with Summer Vegetables over Fettucini.

The custom-built wine cellar is built into the wall with a glass panel to display more than 2,000 bottles from which diners can pick and choose.

FULTON'S CRAB HOUSE'S MENU FOR SIX:

Crab Boursin

Cedar Planked Salmon with Herbs

Key Lime Pie

Crab Boursin

Place cheese in a mixing bowl. Mix 3 to 5 minutes on medium speed until smooth. Add all ingredients and mix again until smooth and well blended. Do not overmix. Serve with a variety of crackers or use as a sandwich spread.

Serves 6
Preparation Time:
  5 Minutes

3 lbs. cream cheese, softened
1 cup roasted garlic purée
3½ Tbsps. scallions, chopped
½ cup fresh basil, chopped
3½ oz. lemon juice
1¾ Tbsps. horseradish
3½ Tbsps. crab base
3½ Tbsps. roasted red pepper, diced fine
½ oz. hickory smoked mustard

Cedar Planked Salmon with Herbs

Serves 4
Preparation Time:
Preheat oven to 375°

- 2 **cloves garlic, chopped fine**
- 2 **Tbsps. olive oil**
- 2 **Tbsps. smoked mustard**
- 2½ **lbs. salmon filet, skinless, boneless**
- 3 **fresh thyme sprigs**
- 3 **fresh rosemary sprigs**
- 6 to 8 **fresh sage leaves**
- 1 **Tbsp. sea salt**
  Cracked black pepper to taste

P lace cedar plank in oven to heat. Chop garlic or press through a garlic press. Mix with olive oil and mustard. Brush over both sides of salmon. Chop herbs coarsely. Sprinkle herbs and seasonings on both sides of salmon. Remove plank from oven. Place salmon filet on plank. Return to oven and cook until fish is opaque when tested with fork. Remove from oven.

Serve with vegetables.

Key Lime Pie

For the crust: Beat butter with mixer until soft. Add sugar, cinnamon and baking powder. Mix well. Add the egg and vanilla. Then add graham cracker crumbs and hazelnuts, then flour. Mix until just blended. Press onto sides and bottom of a greased springform pan. Bake at 350° for 10 minutes. Remove and cool to room temperature.

For the filling: Mix all ingredients together, beating until smooth, and pour into prebaked pie crust. Place back into oven for 15 more minutes at 350°. Remove from oven and cool completely.

Garnish with whipped topping flavored with Key lime juice.

Serves 6
Preparation Time:
  30 Minutes
Preheat oven to 350°

Crust:

  5 oz. unsalted butter
  ½ cup granulated sugar
  2 tsps. cinnamon
  2 tsps. baking powder
  1 egg
  ¼ tsp. vanilla
  ½ cup graham cracker
    crumbs
  ¾ cup hazelnuts, ground
  2¼ cups flour

Filling:

  10 egg yolks
  28 oz. sweetened
    condensed milk
  9 oz. Key lime juice

MAISON AND JARDIN

CONTINENTAL CUISINE
430 South Wymore Road
Altamonte Springs, Florida 32714
(407) 862-4410
Dinner Monday–Saturday 6PM–10PM
Dinner Sunday 6PM–9PM
Brunch Sunday 11AM–2PM
Average Dinner for Two: $75

Maison and Jardin began serving the public in 1958, but it wasn't until owner Bill Beuret purchased the five-acre property in 1971 that it became one of Florida's finest restaurants. The neoclassical architecture was inspired by a mansion in the south of France dating back to Roman times. Guests enjoy the unique design of each dining room. The Gazebo Room evokes the feel of a Mediterranean chateau with hand-painted tile walls overlooking a tiered fountain, waterfall and goldfish pond. Or maybe the Patio Room with its air canvas roof and brick floor. Throughout the restaurant, you will find Oriental rugs, Austrian crystal and antique mirrors in frames from a 17th century Venetian palazzo.

As a Wine Spectator Grand Award winner, Maison and Jardin's wine list is recognized as one of the world's finest. There is a bottle to complement everything on the menu, including buffalo.

MAISON AND JARDIN'S MENU FOR FOUR:

Savory Wild Mushrooms

Wild Rice Bisque

Spring Salad with Basil Vinaigrette

Snapper Maison

Bananas Foster

Savory Wild Mushrooms

Heat clarified butter in skillet. Sauté shallots. Add rosemary, thyme, shiitake and oyster mushrooms and sauté for about 3 minutes. Pour in brandy and flame it. Add heavy cream and simmer for approximately 5 minutes. Thicken with diluted cornstarch. Season to taste.

Divide the mushroom mixture and sauce over the toast rounds and top with cheese slices. Glaze under top broiler until browned and warm. Garnish with rosemary sprigs and serve.

Serves 6
Preparation Time:
   25 Minutes

   2 oz. clarified butter
   2 tsps. shallots
   2 tsps. fresh rosemary, chopped
1½ tsps. fresh thyme, chopped
   2 oz. shiitake mushrooms, diced
   2 oz. oyster mushrooms, diced
   2 oz. brandy
   2 cups heavy cream
   2 Tbsps. cornstarch diluted in cold water
   Salt and pepper to taste
 12 toast rounds
 12 slices of fontina cheese
 12 rosemary sprigs for garnish

Wild Rice Bisque

Serves 12
Preparation Time:
30 Minutes

¼ lb. sweet butter
1 small onion, diced
½ celery stalk, diced
1½ cups sherry
8 cups chicken stock
3 chicken bouillon cubes
3½ cups heavy cream
2½ cups cooked wild rice
2 oz. flour dissolved in
    water
    Salt and pepper to
    taste
¼ tsp. nutmeg

Melt butter over low heat. Sauté onion and celery until translucent. Increase heat and add sherry, chicken stock, chicken bouillon and heavy cream. Bring to a boil. Reduce heat and add nutmeg, rice, salt and pepper. Slowly add flour-water mixture until slightly thickened. Simmer for another 15 minutes and serve.

Spring Salad with Basil Vinaigrette

F or the vinaigrette: Place ingredients in a blender and emulsify.

For the salad: Wash the radicchio, red oak leaf lettuce, frisée, endive and red chicory. Tear into bite-sized pieces and mix together. Add the Basil Vinaigrette Dressing and mix together. Garnish with cheese and pecans.

Serves 6
Preparation Time:
  10 Minutes

Basil Vinaigrette
  Dressing:
Yield: 2 cups
Preparation Time:
  5 Minutes

  1 cup basil, chopped
  ¼ cup red wine vinegar
  ⅛ cup shallots, chopped
    fine
  ¾ cup extra virgin olive
    oil
  ½ tsp. Dijon mustard
    Salt and pepper to
    taste

Salad:
Preparation Time:
  5 Minutes

  ½ head of radicchio
  2 heads red oak leaf
    lettuce
  2 heads frisée
  1 head endive
  2 heads red chicory
  ¾ cup Basil Vinaigrette
    Dressing
  2 oz. chèvre cheese
  2 oz. pecans, chopped
    coarsely

Snapper Maison

Serves 4
Preparation Time:
  40 Minutes
Preheat oven to 425°

Stuffing:

  8 oz. crab meat,
     shredded (preferably
     king or snow crab;
     make sure there are no
     shells)
  ¾ cup mayonnaise
  1 tsp. dry mustard
  1 tsp. Worcestershire
     sauce
     Juice from ½ lemon
  1 Tbsp. capers, copped
     Salt to taste

Snapper:

  4 snapper filets, skinned,
     6 oz. each
  4 puff dough sheets,
     rolled ⅛-inch thick,
     5 inches by 5 inches
  1 egg
  1 oz. water

F or the stuffing: Gently mix all ingredients together.
Top each snapper fillet with 2 oz. crab meat mixture. Wrap crab-topped fish in puff pastry with the seam at the bottom.

Beat the egg and water together to create an egg wash. Brush on puff dough. Bake at 425° for approximately 20 minutes.

Bananas Foster

I n a sauté pan, melt the butter and add the sugar. Cook until caramelized.

Add cinnamon, banana liqueur and syrup to butter mixture and mix well.

Peel and slice each banana in half lengthwise, then cut each half into thirds. Place in the pan with the sauce and strain lemon juice over the banana. Cook until the bananas begin to soften. Turn bananas over and continue cooking to ensure they are cooked thoroughly. If the sauce boils before the bananas are cooked, reduce the heat and continue cooking.

Gather the bananas and sauce to one side of the pan. Hold the pan partly away from the burner with the side of the pan that does not have the bananas and sauce close to the flame. As the residue starts to bubble, it is hot enough to flame the rum. Remove the pan from the flame, pour the rum onto that side of the pan and return the pan to the heat. The rum will ignite. Be careful to remove the pan from the flame before adding the rum to the pan.

Place a scoop of ice cream in the center of each serving plate. Place three banana slices around the ice cream and spoon the sauce over all.

Serves 4
Preparation Time:
  30 Minutes

  3 oz. butter
  ¼ cup sugar
    Cinnamon to taste
  2 oz. banana liqueur
  1 Tbsp. molasses or
    maple syrup
  2 bananas
    Juice from 1 lemon,
    strained
1½ oz. white rum
  4 scoops vanilla ice
    cream

PARK PLAZA GARDENS

CONTEMPORARY AMERICAN CUISINE
319 Park Avenue South
Winter Park, Florida 32789
(407) 645-2475
Lunch Monday–Saturday 11:30AM–2PM
Dinner Monday–Thursday 6PM–10PM
Dinner Friday–Sunday 6PM–9PM
Brunch Sunday 11AM–3PM
Average Dinner for Two: $70

Located in historic Winter Park, Park Plaza Gardens has been ranked one of the top restaurants in Florida since it opened in 1979. The dining room seems to be a fresh-air courtyard with brick floors, beautiful live trees and tropical plants, but with a glass roof that encloses the New Orleans-style patio and allows for year-round dining. Diners can enjoy lunch with the sun shining through the roof, flooding the garden with light. At night, with the stars up above, the candlelight dining room exudes a romantic air.

Executive Chef Christopher Street and Sous Chef Christopher Andrew have recently unveiled a new menu they feel sure will please any palate. They enjoy learning new ways to utilize the native products of Florida. Together, they are creating a lighter, more tropically focused cuisine.

Some of the mouth-watering entrées to try are the Pan-Seared Shrimp and Penne Pasta with Sun-Dried Tomato, Eggplant and Arugula, Katafi-Crusted Salmon Served with Curried Saffron Risotto, Vegetable Spring Rolls, Wild Mushroom and Crab and Smoked Mozzarella Omelet.

PARK PLAZA GARDEN'S MENU FOR FOUR:

Pan-Seared Foie Gras with Champagne Sauce

Apple and Brie Soup

Oven-Roasted Goat Cheese Salad

West Indian Salmon

Grand Marnier Soufflé

Pan-Seared Foie Gras with Champagne Sauce

Melt ¼ cup butter in a small saucepan over low heat. Add the shallots and cook them until they turn golden brown. Next add in the champagne and bay leaves. Let this mixture reduce until only 4 cups remain.

Strain through a fine chinois and return mixture to the saucepan. Over very low heat, whisk in the remaining butter. Add in the grapes and season with salt and pepper to taste. Set mixture aside.

Season the foie gras liberally with salt and white pepper and then dust with flour. Cook the foie gras in a smoking hot sauté pan until it is golden brown on all sides. Place the foie gras in a 400° oven for 4 minutes.

While the foie gras is cooking, warm up the champagne sauce and spoon it onto a plate. When the foie gras is done, place it atop the sauce.

Serve with toast points if desired.

Serves 4
Preparation Time:
  30 Minutes
Preheat oven to 400°

- 2 cups butter, softened
- 4 tsps. shallots
- 12 cups champagne
- 4 bay leaves
- 1 cup champagne grapes, stemmed
  Salt and pepper to taste
- 12 oz. Hudson Valley foie gras
- 1 cup flour

★

Apple and Brie Soup

Serves 4
Preparation Time:
20 Minutes

  1 **cup butter**
  1 **cup flour**
  1 **tsp. salt**
  4 **cups milk**
16 **cups brie, diced small**
  4 **cups apple juice**
  2 **Granny Smith apples,**
    peeled, cored, diced
    small (squeeze some
    lemon juice over the
    apples to keep them
    from oxidizing)

elt the butter in a saucepan over low heat. Blend in flour and salt. Gradually add in the milk, whisking constantly until thickened. Add in the brie and stir until the cheese has melted. Add the juice and the apples and let steep for 15 minutes.

Oven-Roasted Goat Cheese Salad

Mix the first 7 ingredients in a large mixing bowl. Form mixture into 4-oz. balls. Place each ball on a slice of toasted French baguette. Place on a cookie sheet and heat for 4 minutes in a 350° oven. Remove from oven and place over your favorite greens (preferably utilizing a slightly bitter green). Drizzle with olive oil and balsamic vinegar to taste.

Serves 4
Preparation Time:
  15 Minutes
Preheat oven to 350°

  1 **lb. goat cheese**
  ¼ **cup pine nuts, toasted**
  1 **Tbsp. fresh cilantro,**
     finely chopped
  1 **Tbsp. fresh thyme,**
     finely chopped
  1 **tsp. fresh rosemary,**
     finely chopped
     Kosher salt to taste
     Black pepper to taste
  4 **baguette slices, toasted**
  ¼ **cup extra-virgin olive**
     oil
  4 **Tbsps. balsamic**
     vinegar

★

West Indian Salmon

Serves 4
Preparation Time:
30 Minutes
Preheat oven to 350°

1 lb. salmon
Salt and white pepper
to taste
½ cup horseradish root,
grated
¼ cup pickled
horseradish
½ tsp. thyme
½ tsp. parsley
1 cup bread crumbs
Flour for dusting
1 egg for egg wash
Peanut oil for sautéing

Season salmon with salt and pepper. Combine horse-radish root, pickled horseradish, thyme, parsley and bread crumbs. Dust salmon with flour, dip in egg wash, then in bread crumb mix on the top side only.

Heat oil in sauté pan until smoking hot, add salmon, bread-crumbed side down, and sauté for 30 seconds. Finish cooking in a 350° oven for 8 minutes.

★

Grand Marnier Soufflé

Grease soufflé cups with butter and sprinkle lightly with sugar.

Melt butter in a small saucepan over low heat. Remove from heat and add in the flour and salt and mix until smooth. Add the milk a little at a time, making sure to stir constantly. Return to heat.

Beat the egg yolks until thick. Add the hot cream sauce a little at a time, whipping constantly until all the sauce has been added. Set aside to cool.

Beat all 8 egg whites until soft peaks form. Add sugar gradually, beating constantly until soft peaks form. Gradually beat in the lemon juice, a few drops at a time. Stir the Grand Marnier and orange zest into the egg yolk mixture, stirring well. Add all at once to the egg whites, folding thoroughly. Divide the mixture evenly between the soufflé dishes and set dishes in a water bath. Bake for 30 minutes. Remove from oven and serve immediately.

Serves 4
Preparation Time:
45 Minutes
Preheat oven to 350°

4 soufflé cups, 5-oz. each
  Butter for greasing
  Sugar for dusting
⅓ cup butter
¾ cup flour
½ tsp. salt
1½ cups milk
5 eggs, separated
3 egg whites
1 cup sugar
2 Tbsps. lemon juice
½ cup Grand Marnier
1 tsp. orange rind, grated

PORTOBELLO YACHT CLUB

NORTHERN ITALIAN CUISINE
Pleasure Island
1650 Buena Vista Drive
Lake Buena Vista, Florida 32802
(407) 934-8888
Daily 11:30AM–Midnight
Average Dinner For Two: $45

Portobello Yacht Club transports guests to "a sunny day on the Italian Riviera," celebrating good food and good wine. The interior reflects this feeling with its bright colors and terra cotta accents.

Chef Pollack is considered to be one of the best seafood chefs in the country. He enjoys the challenge of developing seasonal dishes using fresh local ingredients.

A winner of a myriad of awards, Portobello Yacht Club specializes in contemporary Italian cuisine that reflects the ingredients and palates of the country's various regions, especially the north. The recipes they have shared with us are their most popular signature dishes.

Their wine cellar, which has won Wine Spectator's Award of Excellence, includes well-chosen wines from Italy and California.

PORTOBELLO YACHT CLUB'S MENU FOR TWO:

Funghi alla Portobello

Farfalle Primavera

Seafood Spaghettini

Costoletta de Maiale

White Chocolate Crème Brûlé

Funghi alla Portobello

Scrape off the gills from the mushrooms. Mix all ingredients for marinade together and mix well. Rub mushrooms with marinade. Place on sheet tray and roast or grill until done. Place arugula on center of plate. Lay mushrooms on their sides. Drizzle with vinaigrette. Sprinkle with onions and Parmigiano-Reggiano.

For the vinaigrette: Place all ingredients in a blender or food processor and purée well.

Serves 2
Preparation Time:
30 Minutes

- 6 oz. portobello mushrooms
  Marinade (recipe follows)
- 2 oz. Tomato Vinaigrette (recipe follows)
- 1 oz. arugula
- ¼ oz. Parmigiano-Reggiano cheese, shaved
- ½ oz. red onions, shaved

Marinade:

- ¼ oz. garlic, chopped
- ¼ oz. fresh rosemary, chopped
- ½ oz. olive oil
  Salt and pepper to taste

Tomato Vinaigrette:

- 1 fresh plum tomato
- 3 fresh basil leaves
- ½ oz. extra virgin olive oil
  Salt and pepper to taste
- ¼ oz. balsamic vinegar

☆

Farfalle Primavera

Serves 4 to 6
Preparation Time:
  25 Minutes

  2 lbs. bow-tie pasta
     (farfalle)
  4 oz. clarified butter
  4 oz. fresh asparagus, cut
     diagonally
  4 oz. snow pea pods
  3 cups heavy whipping
     cream
  8 oz. imported
     Parmesan cheese
     Salt and white pepper
     to taste
  1 or 2 sun-dried
     tomatoes

I n boiling water, cook pasta until al dente. Meanwhile, place clarified butter in hot sauté pan. Add asparagus pieces and cook slightly. Add in snow peas and toss. Add cream, cheese, salt and pepper. Place in pasta bowls. Sprinkle with tomatoes for color. Serve immediately.

☆

Shellfish Spaghettini

Peel and devein shrimp. Scrub mussels and clams. Clean scallops if they still have adductor muscles attached. Cut crab.

Bring water to a boil. Cook pasta until al dente. Drain, rinse and set aside.

Heat olive oil in a large sauté pan. Add clams and mussels tossing gently 2 to 3 minutes. Add garlic and allow to brown to golden. Add remaining seafood and toss well 1 to 2 minutes. Do not allow garlic to burn. Add wine. Add tomatoes, pasta and herbs. Toss well, allowing flavors to blend.

When shrimp are cooked through, and all the shellfish are open, pasta is ready. Add salt and pepper to taste. Divide pasta into bowls.

Serves 4
Preparation Time:
  30 Minutes

  8 shrimp, peeled,
    deveined
  8 to 10 mussels,
    scrubbed, debearded
10 to 12 littleneck clams,
    scrubbed
¾ lb. fresh scallops
¾ lb. crab legs, cut into
    2-inch segments
  1 lb. spaghettini pasta
¼ cup olive oil
  1 Tbsp. garlic, crushed
½ cup dry white wine
  2 cans imported Italian
    tomatoes
  2 Tbsps. basil, chopped
  1 Tbsp. Italian parsley,
    chopped
    Salt and pepper to
    taste

☆

Costoletta di Maiale

Serves 2
Preparation Time:
  20 Minutes
(note marinating time)

¼ oz. fresh rosemary,
  chopped
¼ oz. garlic, chopped
½ oz. olive oil
  Salt and pepper to
  taste
2 pork chops, 7 oz. each
2 oz. chicken stock
  Roasted garlic mashed
  potatoes
  Vegetables
  Parsley sprigs for
  garnish

ix together rosemary, garlic, olive oil, salt and pepper. Coat pork chops with the mixture and marinate overnight.

Place marinated pork chops in a hot pan. Cook until medium-well done. Add chicken stock and let reduce by half.

Serve with roasted garlic mashed potatoes and vegetables. Pour the reduction over and around chops and garnish with parsley sprigs.

☆

White Chocolate Crème Brûlé

Position rack in center of oven.
Whisk egg yolks and ¼ cup of sugar in a medium bowl.

Bring cream and remaining sugar to a simmer in a heavy saucepan. Reduce heat to low. Gradually add the chocolate to the cream mixture and whisk until smooth. Gradually whisk chocolate mixture into yolk mixture. Mix in vanilla. Ladle custard into four 10-oz. custard cups.

Place cups in a large baking pan. Add enough hot water to pan to come halfway up sides of cups. Bake until custards are set in the center, about 1 hour. Remove custards from water and cool. Cover and refrigerate overnight.

Preheat broiler. Sprinkle ½ Tbsp. of sugar over each custard. Broil until sugar caramelizes, watching carefully, about 2 minutes. Serve hot, or refrigerate up to 1 hour and serve cold.

Serves 4
Preparation Time:
 1½ Hours
(note refrigeration time)
Preheat oven to 300°

 5 **large egg yolks**
½ **cup sugar**
 2 **cups whipping cream**
 3 **oz. imported fine**
   white chocolate, finely
   chopped
¼ **tsp. vanilla extract**
 2 **Tbsps. sugar**

☆

BAYBORO HOUSE

1719 Beach Drive Southeast
St. Petersburg, Florida 33701
(813) 823-4955
Room Rates: $85–$120

Voted among the best bed and breakfasts in the state of Florida, Bayboro House extends a warm invitation to guests to step back into a more tranquil time. The historical waterfront bed and breakfast is decorated with beautiful furnishings that have been collected over the years by proprietors Gordon and Antonia Powers. Complimentary wine is served in the parlor each evening or on the verandah, complete with swing, rockers, chaise and wicker chairs.

Each of the guest rooms offers a private bathroom, air conditioning, television and a morning newspaper at your door.

Breakfast specialties served in the formal dining room include freshly squeezed orange juice, fresh fruits, hot rolls and muffins. The Bayboro House its guests will savor the old-fashioned hospitality and stay awhile.

Banana Bread

I n a bowl, mix all the ingredients together. Pour into a 9 × 5-inch loaf pan that has been greased and floured. Bake at 325° for approximately 1 hour or until a toothpick comes out clean.

Cooking Secret: This bread is delicious with cream cheese.

Yield: 1 loaf
Preparation Time:
  5 Minutes
Preheat oven to 325°

  1¾ cups flour
  1½ cups sugar
   1 tsp. baking soda
   2 eggs, beaten
   2 to 3 ripe bananas,
     mashed
  ½ cup oil
  ¼ cup buttermilk
   1 tsp. vanilla extract
  ½ cup walnuts, optional

☆

BELLEVIEW MIDO RESORT HOTEL

25 Belleview Boulevard
Clearwater, Florida 34617
(800) 237-8947
(813) 442-6171
Room Rates: $150–$450

With its renowned elegance, the Belleview Mido Resort Hotel overlooks the intracoastal waters in a prestigious area of Florida's West Coast. Here, in a private setting of velvet lawns and tree-lined paths, you can indulge in a wide variety of leisure activities. Play tennis on all-weather, red clay courts. Unwind with a massage, sauna or facial at the spa and fitness club. Enjoy a challenging round of golf on the 18-hole, par 72 championship course.

The Belleview Mido offers an inviting choice of guest accommodations that include cozy sun parlors and charming balcony suites, with all the first-class amenities.

Within the resort, there are unique shops, charming boutiques and a world-class art gallery. With six restaurants and lounges, there is a place for every palate and mood.

Ossobuco alla Milanese

In a wide, shallow pan over medium heat, combine the butter and ½ garlic clove.

In a separate bowl, flour the veal.

When the garlic begins to brown, discard it and add the veal. Brown the meat on both sides. Reduce the heat, cover the pan and cook slowly, adding a few spoonfuls of white wine or meat stock from time to time. Cook for about 1½ hours, turning the pieces to make sure they cook evenly and become golden brown all over. Season with salt and pepper.

Meanwhile, chop the remaining garlic with the parsley and lemon peel. When the meat is done, sprinkle the parsley mixture and the lemon juice over it and cook for another 10 minutes.

Serve the veal with the cooking juices drizzled over it.

Serves 4
Preparation Time:
  2 Hours

  3 Tbsps. butter
  1 clove garlic
  4 veal shank chunks,
      12 oz. each
      Flour for dusting
  1 cup dry white wine or
      meat stock
      Salt and pepper to
      taste
  1 parsley sprig
      Rind and juice from ½
      lemon, grated

Chicken alla Cacciatore

Serves 4
Preparation Time:
1 Hour

  1 small chicken
     Salt and pepper to
     taste
     Flour for dusting
  2 Tbsps. butter
  2 Tbsps. olive oil
  1 onion, chopped
  1 bouquet garni
  ½ cup dry white wine
1½ cups fresh mushrooms,
     sliced
  3 tomatoes, peeled,
     seeded, coarsely
     chopped
  1 Tbsp. parsley
  3 cups any stock

Cut the chicken into 4 pieces, removing the bones. Add salt and pepper and dust with flour.

In a heavy skillet over medium heat, melt the butter with the olive oil. Add the onion, bouquet garni and chicken pieces. Brown on all sides.

Add the wine and cook for about 10 minutes. Add the mushrooms, tomatoes, parsley and stock. Cover the skillet and simmer for 45 minutes, or until tender. If necessary, add a small amount of hot water.

Crème Caramel

Warm a 1½ qt. soufflé dish in a pan of hot water so it will not crack when you add the caramel syrup.

To make the syrup, pour 1 cup sugar into a heavy skillet. Cook over medium heat until the sugar begins to melt, about 5 minutes. Stir with a wooden spoon until the sugar is completely melted and golden brown.

Remove the soufflé dish from the water and immediately pour in the caramel syrup. Hold the dish with pot holders and rotate it until the bottom and sides are thoroughly coated with syrup. Set aside.

Heat the milk to just below scalding. Set aside.

Beat the eggs and egg yolks together. Add the remaining sugar and beat until well combined, but do not overbeat or you will have air bubbles in the custard. Add the vanilla. While stirring constantly, slowly add the hot milk to the egg and sugar mixture.

Pour the mixture into the caramel-lined soufflé dish. Place the soufflé dish in a shallow pan and pour boiling water into the pan until it reaches halfway up the soufflé dish.

Bake for 1 hour or until a knife inserted in the center of the custard comes out clean. Remove custard from the oven and chill until ready to serve.

To unmold, run a small knife around the edge of the dish to loosen the custard. Place a serving dish upside-down over the custard; then quickly invert, shaking gently if necessary.

Serve with whipped cream.

Serves 4
Preparation Time:
1½ Hours
Preheat oven to 325°

1⅔ **cups sugar**
1 **qt. milk**
6 **eggs**
2 **egg yolks**
1½ **tsps. vanilla**
    Whipped cream for
    garnish, optional

☆

CHALET SUZANNE COUNTRY INN AND RESTAURANT

3800 Chalet Suzanne Drive
Lake Wales, Florida 33853-7060
(800) 433-6011
(941) 676-6011
Room Rates: $139–$195

S urrounded by a 70-acre estate, the family-owned Chalet Suzanne Country Inn and Restaurant has been welcoming guests since 1931. This delightful inn of 30 rooms is a gracious oasis amid the attractions of Central Florida.

Each room greets you with a different decor, with a private entrance by either courtyard or patio. Every corner of the inn glows with the charm of stained glass, antiques and old lamps from faraway places.

The restaurant has earned a glowing reputation for its cuisine. Gourmet Magazine called it "glorious." Meals are served in the unique setting of five quaint rooms located on several levels, overlooking the lake. The Soup Cannery is where the inn's delicious soups are processed to be shipped all over the world. The soups have even been eaten on the moon.

Broiled Grapefruit

S lice grapefruit in half and cut membrane around center of fruit. Cut around each section half, close to membrane, so that the fruit is completely loosened from its shell.

Fill the center of each half with 1½ Tbsps. butter. Sprinkle ½ tsp. sugar over each half, then sprinkle each with 2 Tbsps. cinnamon-sugar mixture.

Place grapefruit on a shallow baking pan and broil just long enough to brown tops and heat to bubbling.

Remove from the oven and serve hot.

Serves 2
Preparation Time:
  10 Minutes

1 grapefruit, room
  temperature
3 Tbsps. butter
1 tsp. sugar
4 Tbsps. cinnamon-sugar
  mix (1 part cinnamon
  to 4 parts sugar)

COLONY BEACH AND TENNIS RESORT

1620 Gulf of Mexico Drive
Longboat Key, Florida 34228-3499
(800) 4-COLONY
(941) 383-6464
Room Rates: $180–$975

Fresh flowers and tropical plants welcome you to an elegant suite, beautifully decorated with lovely furnishings and fabrics. Each has a living room, dining area, one or two private bedrooms, a European-style kitchen, a marble bath, sun balcony and daily maid service.

The Colony Beach and Tennis Resort is one of the jewels of the Florida landscape. Voted the best tennis resort in the nation by National Tennis Magazine, it also offers an expansive private beach, fitness center, health spa and award-winning dining.

The Colony Restaurant, overlooking the Gulf of Mexico, is a gourmet's delight, offering a lavish menu. The extensive wine cellar has received national and international praise. The mini-grocery market, Tastebuds, offers everything to stock your vacation refrigerator, from milk and bread, wine and liquor, to a variety of delicious entrées, sandwiches, salads and pâté prepared by the Colony Restaurant. For your added convenience, you can have the items delivered to your suite just prior to your arrival.

Oriental Salmon Tartare

Grind or chop the salmon and place in a medium-sized bowl.

In a separate bowl, combine the onion, capers, cilantro, oil and lemon juice. Season with Tabasco, salt and pepper. Fold all ingredients together until combined. Adjust seasonings to taste and chill.

Spread a thin layer of wasabi on each wonton, mound the salmon tartare on the wonton and drizzle with sesame oil.

Garnish with flying fish roe and cilantro sprigs.

Yield: 15 pieces
Preparation Time:
20 Minutes

½ lb. fresh salmon filet
1 red onion, diced small
¼ cup capers, chopped
1 Tbsp. fresh cilantro, chopped
1 Tbsp. extra-virgin olive oil
2 Tbsps. lemon juice
  Tabasco Sauce to taste
  Salt and pepper to taste
¼ cup wasabi paste
15 wonton skins, fried
  Sesame oil to taste
  Japanese tobikko or flying fish roe for garnish (optional)
  Cilantro sprigs for garnish

Shrimp and Sea Scallop Grand Marnier with Orzo Pasta

Serves 4
Preparation Time:
  25 Minutes

20 Gulf shrimp, 16/20 size,
   deveined, tails on
16 large sea scallops
   Salt and pepper to
   taste
   Extra-virgin olive oil
   for sautéing
 1 Tbsp. shallots, chopped
¼ cup Grand Marnier
⅓ cup orange juice
 2 Valencia oranges,
   separated into
   segments
 4 Tbsps. butter, cut into
   pieces
20 to 24 oz. orzo and
   ricotta (recipe follows)
¼ cup almond halves,
   toasted, for garnish
 2 Tbsps. parsley,
   chopped, for garnish

Orzo and Ricotta:

 1 lb. imported orzo pasta
¼ cup clarified butter
 2 Tbsps. heavy cream
¼ cup chicken stock
 3 oz. ricotta (sheep milk
   ricotta preferred)
 2 Tbsps. orange juice
 1 tsp. orange zest
   Salt and pepper to
   taste

Season the shrimp and scallops with salt and pepper, then sauté in olive oil until almost cooked through. Add the shallots, then deglaze the pan with Grand Marnier.

Add the orange juice and reduce for 3 minutes. Add the orange segments and cook for 1 minute.

Whip in the butter pieces to create a smooth sauce.

Arrange, alternating shrimp and scallops around ¾ cup of orzo in the center of each serving plate. Drizzle with sauce and garnish with almonds and parsley.

For the orzo and ricotta: Cook the orzo pasta according to directions on the box. Drain.

Heat the clarified butter, then add the orzo and stir to combine. Add cream and chicken stock and heat through. Fold in the cheese, orange juice and zest. Season with salt and pepper to taste.

Curry-Dusted Chilean Sea Bass with Mango Ginger Chutney

Combine the vinegar, sugar and ginger together in a small saucepan over medium heat. Bring to a boil. Reduce heat and simmer for 5 minutes.

Add the mangoes and simmer for another 10 minutes. Cool to room temperature.

In a shallow dish combine the curry powder and rice flour. Dredge the filets in the curry-seasoned flour and pan-sear on high heat, approximately 2 minutes on each side. Finish in a 375° oven for 6 minutes.

To serve, paint serving plates and fish with the mango ginger chutney. Garnish with black sesame seeds on the rims of the plates.

Serves 4
Preparation Time:
  30 Minutes
Preheat oven to 375°

¼ cup rice wine vinegar
2 Tbsps. extra-fine granulated sugar
2 Tbsps. fresh ginger root, sliced paper-thin
2 ripe mangoes, diced
4 tsps. curry powder
¼ cup rice flour
4 Chilean sea bass filets (black grouper and mahi mahi also work well)
2 Tbsps. extra-virgin olive oil
  Black sesame seeds for garnish (optional)

☆

DREAMSPINNER BED AND BREAKFAST

117 Diedrich Street
Eustis, Florida 32726
(888) 479-1229
(352) 589-8082
Room Rates: $105–$115

A wraparound porch welcomes you to this charming bed and breakfast and its surrounding gardens filled with moss-laden oaks and romantically shaded benches and ponds. Antique roses, camellias and azaleas embellish over an acre of grounds. Elegant English fabrics adorn the well-appointed rooms. Art, antiques and fireplaces provide an eclectic, comfortable setting.

The historical integrity of the Dreamspinner has been maintained, along with modern amenities for your comfort. The Victorian house, now called the Dreamspinner, was built in 1881. The kitchen and servants' quarters were originally separated from the main house by a breezeway, which now connects the two dwellings.

Your day will begin with a generous breakfast of homemade breads, jams and freshly brewed coffee. In the afternoon enjoy traditional English tea, followed later by wine and cheese each evening. Relax and enjoy the peace and tranquillity, or venture to nearby attractions such as Disney World, golf, tennis, antique shopping, fishing, horseback riding, or a visit to the Ocala National Forest.

Chicken Salad

Marinate the cooked chicken in lemon juice for 1 hour. Add the celery, grapes and almonds, mixing well. In a separate bowl, combine the dry mustard with the cream, blending to a smooth consistency. Add salt, pepper and mayonnaise and mix thoroughly.

Add the sauce to the chicken mixture. Chill before serving.

Cooking Secret: This recipe is delicious with chilled asparagus or fresh fruit or in a pineapple boat.

Serves 8
Preparation Time:
  30 Minutes
(note marinating time)

  3 **cups chicken breast,**
    cubed, cooked,
    boneless
  2 **Tbsps. lemon juice**
1½ **cups celery, chopped**
  1 **cup seedless green**
    grapes
  1 **cup almond halves,**
    toasted, blanched
  1 **tsp. dry mustard**
 ¼ **cup light cream**
    Salt and pepper to
    taste
  1 **cup mayonnaise**

GROSVENOR RESORT

Walt Disney World Village
P.O. Box 22202
Lake Buena Vista, Florida 32830-2202
(800) 624-4109
(407) 828-4444
Room Rates: $69–$100

L ocated inside Walt Disney World Village, the Grosvenor Resort is situated on 13 beautifully landscaped lakeside acres. Within walking distance are Pleasure Island and the Disney Village Marketplace.

The Grosvenor Resort offers two heated swimming pools, hot tub, lighted tennis and handball courts, basketball courts, volleyball courts, electronic game room, children's pool, playground and fitness center. The staff is dedicated to old-fashioned service that will make your stay all the more pleasant.

Elegant and comfortable, Baskervilles, the British theme dining room, features an authentic Sherlock Holmes museum—a re-creation of the sleuth's dwelling at 221B Baker Street. The adjoining pub, Moriarty's, named after Holmes' archenemy, offers the revelry of an English pub.

Pineapple Salsa

ix all the ingredients together.
Serve with chips or use as a garnish for poultry and meats.

Yield: About 5 cups
Preparation Time:
  5 Minutes

¼ cup fresh basil leaves, julienned
2 pineapples, finely diced
2 Tbsps. jalapeño peppers, finely diced
2 Tbsps. brown sugar
2 Tbsps. honey
2 Tbsps. white vinegar
½ red onion, finely diced
½ red bell pepper, finely diced
3 Tbsps. pineapple juice

HERITAGE HOTEL AND GRILLE

234 Third Avenue North
St. Petersburg, Florida 33701
(800) 283-7829
(813) 822-4818
Room Rates: $64–$95

A quaint hotel, beautifully appointed in the grand style of the '20s, the Heritage offers guest rooms decorated with the furnishings of the past, combined with all the modern conveniences you'd expect in a fine hotel.

The Heritage is within walking distance of the famous Salvador Dali Museum and the St. Petersburg Museum of Fine Art. The Pier features great shopping, fine food and entertainment. St. Petersburg Thunder Dome is minutes away.

The Heritage Grille, an award-winning fine dining restaurant, is a favorite of locals. Cocktails are served from the bar that once graced Confederate President Jefferson Davis' home.

Grilled Red Snapper with Spicy Mango-Avocado Salsa and Smoked Gouda Quesadilla

Season the fish well and score the skin side. Season with salt and pepper to taste. Grill the fish for 3 to 5 minutes, starting with the flesh side down, in a sauté pan with olive oil. Then turn the fish and cook until done. Remove from pan.

In a large mixing bowl combine the avocados, mangoes, tomatoes, onion, bell pepper, cilantro and lime juice. Refrigerate the salsa for 1 hour.

Place the cheese slices on one half of a tortilla. Fold the other half over the cheese. Grill in a sauté pan with oil.

To serve, cut the grilled tortilla in half to form 2 triangles. Place them on the serving plates in a crossing position. Place the fish on top of the quesadillas and drizzle with the salsa.

Serves 2
Preparation Time:
  30 Minutes
(note refrigeration time)

  2 **snapper filets, 7 oz. each, skin on**
    Salt and pepper to taste
1½ **Tbsps. olive oil**
  2 **ripe avocados, medium diced**
  2 **ripe mangoes, medium diced**
  1 **red tomato, diced small**
  1 **yellow tomato, diced small**
  1 **small red onion, diced small**
  1 **green bell pepper, seeded, diced small**
    Cilantro, chopped fine, to taste
    Juice from 1 lime
 10 **to 16 Gouda cheese slices**
  2 **flour tortillas**
 ½ **Tbsp. oil**

★

JD's Southern Oaks

3800 Country Club Road
Winter Haven, Florida 33881-9292
(941) 293-2335
Room Rates: $95–$175

T ravel up the oak-lined driveway to this Southern mansion built in 1925 which is now a unique bed and breakfast, sitting on 37 acres of beautiful Florida land. With its lush lawns, swings, rope hammocks and gazebos, guests can relax in whatever way they wish—except for the pond. They request that guests do not go swimming in the pond, since it is occupied by alligators.

The house is a white clapboard colonial with wrapping porches and antebellum-style pillars. The rooms are furnished with antiques, stained-glass windows and Italian rose marble.

JD's Southern Oaks offers guests a variety of accommodations. The most intriguing would be The Hay Loft, their newest offering. The suite is in the barn—a true "roll in the hay." It includes its own private hot tub and a sitting room with rocking chairs. The spacious deck overlooks many acres of Florida pasture land.

Early morning coffee is served in the gathering room or on the side porch. A delicious, expanded continental breakfast follows, offering homemade breads, pastries, fresh fruit and a fine selection of teas and coffees.

Orange French Toast

In a mixing bowl, whisk together the eggs, orange juice, milk, sugar, vanilla extract and nutmeg.

In a greased 9 × 13-inch pan, place a single tight-fitting layer of bread slices. Pour egg mixture over the bread. Cover and refrigerate overnight, turning once.

In the morning, pour melted butter evenly over the bread. Sprinkle with pecans.

Bake in a 400° oven for 20 to 25 minutes or until golden brown.

To serve, sprinkle each slice with powdered sugar. Serve with syrup and fresh fruit.

Cooking Secret: To increase the orange taste, melt orange marmalade in the microwave and brush a layer on before serving, then sprinkle with powdered sugar and pecans.

Serves 4
Preparation Time:
  20 Minutes
(note refrigeration time)
Preheat oven to 400°

  4 eggs
²/₃ cup freshly squeezed
   orange juice
¹/₂ cup milk
¹/₄ cup sugar
¹/₂ tsp. vanilla extract
¹/₄ tsp. nutmeg
  1 loaf French bread,
   sliced 1 inch thick
¹/₃ cup butter, melted
¹/₂ cup pecans, chopped
   Powdered sugar for
   garnish
   Maple syrup
   Fresh fruit (optional)

MAGNOLIA INN

347 East Third Avenue
Mount Dora, Florida 32757
(800) 776-2112
(352) 735-3800
Web Site: www.magnolia.cde.com
E-mail: Ljohnson@mail.cde.com
Room Rates: $90–$120

Located in a small town in the heart of Florida, the Magnolia Inn is a historic estate, built around 1926 in downtown Mount Dora. A good choice for romantic getaways, the inn focuses on true Southern hospitality in an elegant setting.

Guests lounge in the hammock by the garden wall, swing under the majestic magnolia trees or unwind in the gazebo spa. Explore the small-town pleasures of quaint antique shops, boutiques and exceptional dining found along flower-box-lined streets.

Breakfast is a hearty affair, offering such entrées as blueberry French toast or eggs Benedict accompanied by fresh breads, seasonal fruit and specialty coffees and teas.

Although Magnolia Inn is located only 25 miles from Orlando, and less than one hour from Disney World and the beaches, you may feel so pampered that you don't want to leave.

Crazy Lemon Muffins

 ombine the flour, sugar, baking powder, baking soda, salt and margarine in a medium-sized bowl. Make a well in the center.

Put the remaining ingredients in a separate bowl and whisk together. Add to the flour mixture and stir until moist.

Spoon into greased muffin tins. Bake for 15 to 20 minutes.

Cooking Secret: If desired, make a glaze by mixing 1 part lemon juice to 5 parts sugar and top the muffins with the glaze.

Yield: 6 muffins
Preparation Time:
   10 Minutes
Preheat oven to 400°

   2 cups flour
   ½ cup sugar
   1 tsp. baking powder
   ½ tsp. baking soda
   ¼ tsp. salt
   3 Tbsps. margarine, melted
   1 tsp. lemon rind or zest, grated
   ¼ cup fresh lemon juice
   2 large eggs
   1 cup low fat lemon yogurt
   1 cup craisins (dried cranberries)
   1 tsp. vanilla flavoring

MELLON PATCH INN

3601 North A1A
North Hutchinson Island, Florida 34949
(800) MLN PTCH
(407) 461-5231
Room Rates: $85–$105

A unique Florida-style bed and breakfast, the Mellon Patch Inn offers an ideal setting with genuine hospitality. If you're an early riser, take your cup of coffee across the road to the beach and catch the first rays from the sunrise over the ocean, or walk to Jack Island State Preserve to view early morning nature.

Each bedroom has a private bath and is individually decorated with hand-painted furniture and walls. The exotic Tropical Paradise Room surrounds you with flora and fauna, captured in rich upholstery and wall paintings. The Seaside Serenity Room is colored in tranquil shades of blues and greens, featuring hand-painted furniture with tropical fish and shells. The Santa Fe Sunset Room is bathed in brilliant hues of sunset, with hand-painted Mexican furniture and accessories.

Blintz Soufflé

Grease an 8-inch square baking pan.
Combine the cottage cheese, cream cheese, butter and sugar in a medium-sized bowl. Add the flour, eggs, lemon juice and baking powder and stir well.

Spoon into the prepared pan and sprinkle with cinnamon.

Bake for 45 minutes or until the soufflé is light brown around the edges and springs back at a touch. Cut into squares.

Cooking Secret: This is excellent with fruit toppings. A quick topping is to mix sliced strawberries with a small amount of orange marmalade. Or use 1 cup frozen blueberries, raspberries, cherries or peaches cooked with ¼ cup orange juice, 1 Tbsp. honey and 1 Tbsp. cornstarch dissolved in 1 Tbsp. cold water. Cook until the color becomes clear and the fruit thickens. It is an inn favorite.

Serves 4
Preparation Time:
  1 Hour
Preheat oven to 350°

  1 lb. cottage cheese
  3 oz. cream cheese,
    softened
  ¼ cup butter or
    margarine, melted
  ⅓ cup sugar
  ½ cup flour
  3 eggs
  ½ tsp. fresh lemon juice
  ½ tsp. baking powder
  ½ tsp. cinnamon

Apple Cake

Serves 10 to 12
Preparation Time:
  1½ Hours
Preheat oven to 350°

1½ cups oil
2 cups sugar
3 eggs, beaten
3 cups flour
1 tsp. salt
1 tsp. cinnamon
1 tsp. baking soda
1 tsp. vanilla extract
3 cups apples, peeled,
  cored, thickly sliced
1 cup walnuts, chopped
1 cup dates, chopped

Beat oil and sugar together in a mixing bowl. Add the eggs and beat until the mixture is creamy.

Sift together the flour, salt, cinnamon and soda. Stir into the batter.

Add the remaining ingredients and stir to blend.

Turn the mixture into a buttered and floured 9-inch angel food tube pan. Bake for 1¼ hours or until done.

Cool in pan and serve.

Chocolate Bread Pudding

Divide the bread cubes evenly among eight ¾-cup custard cups.

Bring half and half to a simmer in a heavy, medium saucepan over medium heat. Remove the saucepan from heat.

Add the chocolate and stir until it is melted and smooth. Add the egg yolks, sugar, vanilla and salt and whisk until well blended.

Pour the chocolate custard over the bread cubes, dividing evenly. Press down on bread cubes with a spoon to saturate bread completely. Let stand at room temperature for 25 minutes.

Cover custard cups loosely with foil. Place in an oven and bake until the puddings are set and a toothpick inserted in the center comes out with some moist chocolate custard, about 30 minutes.

Serve bread pudding warm, topped with a dollop of whipped cream.

Serves 8
Preparation Time:
 1 Hour
Preheat oven to 325°

 6 **cups egg bread,**
   trimmed, ½-inch
   cubes, lightly packed
2½ **cups half and half**
 8 **oz. semisweet**
   chocolate, chopped
 4 **large egg yolks**
 ¼ **cup sugar**
 1 **tsp. vanilla extract**
 ½ **tsp. salt**
   Whipping cream,
   lightly sweetened, for
   garnish

Safety Harbor Resort and Spa

105 North Bayshore Drive
Safety Harbor, Florida 34695
(888) BEST SPA
(813) 726-1161
Room Rates: $129–$1,459

People have been coming to Safety Harbor for rejuvenation since long before it was the "in" thing to do. These mineral springs, revered by local Indians for their remarkable healing powers, were discovered in 1539 by Spanish explorer Hernando de Soto. The springs gained worldwide fame and are the primary source of water for the spa. The 50,000-square-foot spa and fitness center, full-service salon, three pools, fitness classes and Phil Green FILA Tennis Academy are some of the amenities that make this a one-of-a-kind resort.

Located on 22 acres of coastline overlooking the bay, most of the guest rooms have over-sized private terraces and scenic water views.

At the helm of all culinary operations is Executive Chef David Day. He has a penchant for turning the heads and tempting the taste buds of resort guests. Menu offerings of the eclectic and unique variety are the rule rather than the exception. The resort boasts two restaurants—the Main Dining Room offers gourmet spa cuisine, while The Cafe, features New American "fusion" fare.

Purée of Butternut Squash and Pear Soup

I n a baking dish, place the cut butternut squash, skin side up, in 2 inches of water. Bake at 400° until fork-tender, or approximately 45 minutes.

In a large stock pot, sauté the onion, carrots, leeks and celery until onions are translucent. Add the pear brandy and flambé.

Add the pears, honey and chicken stock. Bring to a boil, then reduce heat.

When the squash is fork-tender, peel the skin off and add to the soup pot and continue to simmer for 30 minutes.

Strain the soup and purée the solids in a food processor. Combine the purée with the liquid, add the butter, nutmeg and pepper. Chill.

Garnish each serving with crème fraîche, chopped chives and sliced pears fanned over the top of the soup.

Serves 8
Preparation Time:
  1½ Hours
(note refrigeration time)

  3 lbs. butternut squash, cut in half
  ¼ cup onion, peeled, chopped fine
  ¼ cup carrots, chopped fine
  2 Tbsps. leeks, white part only, peeled, chopped fine
  2 Tbsps. celery, peeled, chopped fine
  ¼ cup pear brandy
  1¼ lbs. Bartlett pears, peeled, cored, sliced (save some for garnish)
  ½ cup honey
  3 qts. chicken stock
  1 Tbsp. butter
  ½ tsp. ground nutmeg
  ¼ tsp. cayenne pepper
  ½ cup crème fraîche
  ½ bunch chives, chopped fine

Pan-Seared Salmon Cakes with Sour Cream Chive Sauce, Baby Lettuces and Ginger Lime Vinaigrette

Serves 4 to 6
Preparation Time:
1¾ Hours
(note refrigeration time)
Preheat oven to 350°

1¼ lbs. fresh Norwegian
   salmon filet
¼ cup water
1 bunch scallions, diced
½ cup mayonnaise
¼ cup soy sauce
2 eggs
2 Tbsps. ginger or
   pickled ginger, minced
1 Tbsp. chili paste with
   garlic
¾ cup Japanese bread
   crumbs
½ cup vegetable oil
1 cup sour cream
1 bunch chives, chopped
   fine
Salt and pepper to
   taste
Juice of 6 limes
1 tsp. fresh ginger,
   minced
½ cup vegetable oil
¾ lb. baby lettuce mix

Sauce:

1 cup sour cream
1 bunch chives, chopped
   fine
Salt and pepper

lace fish in a pan and add the water. Bake in a 350° oven for 10 to 15 minutes or until done. Refrigerate fish until cool enough to handle.

In a mixing bowl combine the scallions, mayonnaise, soy sauce, eggs, ginger, chili paste and bread crumbs. Add the cooled salmon to the mixture, blending until well incorporated. Place in the refrigerator for 10 to 15 minutes.

Remove and shape into 2 oz. balls. Dredge in more bread crumbs. Flatten to disk shape and pan fry in vegetable oil until honey-brown in color. Set aside.

Whisk the lime juice and ginger together. Slowly add the vegetable oil constantly whisking until emulsified.

Toss baby lettuce with the vinaigrette and top with salmon cakes dotted with sour cream sauce.

For the sauce: Place sour cream in mixing bowl and add chives. Mix well. Season to taste with salt and pepper.

Low-Fat Applesauce Cheesecake

In a medium-sized bowl, combine the graham crackers, margarine and honey, mixing well. Press into the bottom of an ungreased 10-inch cake pan.

In a large bowl, beat the cream cheese and sugar at medium speed until smooth and creamy. Add the flour and blend well.

At a low speed, add the eggs, one at a time, beating just until blended. Add the applesauce, cinnamon and nutmeg and beat until well blended.

Pour into the crust-lined pan.

Bake at 350° in a water bath for 50 to 60 minutes or until the center is set. Cool completely. Refrigerate several hours or overnight.

Yield: 10-inch cake
Preparation Time:
  30 Minutes
(note refrigeration time)
Preheat oven to 350°

1¼ cups fat-free graham
    crackers, broken up
1½ Tbsps. reduced-fat
    margarine, cubed
1½ Tbsps. honey
1½ lbs. fat-free cream
    cheese, softened
  1 cup sugar
  2 Tbsps. flour
  3 eggs
  1 cup applesauce
  ½ tsp. cinnamon
  ⅛ tsp. nutmeg

THURSTON HOUSE

851 Lake Avenue
Maitland, Florida 32751
(800) 843-2721
(407) 539-1991
E-mail: jball54@aol.com
Room Rates: $100–$110

Nestled in the heart of a five-acre parcel of beautiful wooded land, Thurston House overlooks tranquil Lake Eulalia. Stroll the lovely grounds, where fruit trees, flowering bushes and herb and flower gardens abound.

Built in 1885, the Thurston House has been restored to its original splendor. The woodwork of pine and cypress gleams with wainscoting in the dining room and original hardwood floors throughout.

Curl up in one of the four cozy guest rooms, each named after a former family member. All rooms have a private bath, desk with phone and reading area. A bountiful expanded continental breakfast is served in the dining room each morning.

Orange Bread

In a large bowl, sift together the dry ingredients. Cut in the butter. Add the milk, orange juice, orange marmalade, rind and egg. Beat until well mixed.

Bake at 375° in a greased loaf pan for 50 to 60 minutes. Remove and let cool before slicing.

Yield: 1 loaf
Preparation Time:
 1 Hour
Preheat oven to 375°

2 cups flour
2½ tsps. baking powder
⅛ cup sugar
2 Tbsps. butter, softened
½ cup milk
⅓ cup orange juice
⅔ cup orange marmalade
  Rind from 1 orange, grated
1 large egg, beaten

☆

CAFÉ C'RIZMA

CONTEMPORARY AMERICAN CUISINE
3218 South Atlantic Avenue
Daytona Beach Shores, Florida 32118
(904) 767-3080
Lunch Tuesday–Friday 11:30AM–2PM
Dinner Tuesday–Thursday 5PM–9PM
Dinner Friday and Saturday 5PM–10PM
Average Dinner for Two: $50

Café C'rizMa is a creative blend of the owners' names, Mary and Christian Thormose. And the creativity is extended to every corner and detail of this popular restaurant. A combination art gallery/cafe, this showpiece for the Thormoses allows each to show off their talent in their medium—Chef Christian with food and Mary with music. Every Friday and Saturday night you will find Mary entertaining diners with various medleys from the past and the present.

The eclectic menu incorporates European, Asian and even Indian styles of cooking. Popular entrée highlights are Salmon Napoleon with Boursin Cream, Spinach and Herbed Champagne Sauce, Chicken and Shrimp Curaçao with Green Onions, Coconut and Tomato and Indian Spiced Lamb Kabobs served with Chutney. Dessert favorites are Crêpe Shells Stuffed with Strawberries and Romanoff Sauce and Chèvre Cheesecake in a Hazelnut Crust Drizzled with a Danish Cherry Sauce.

CAFÉ C'RIZMA'S MENU FOR EIGHT:

Cuban Black Bean Soup

Green Salad with Orange Vinaigrette

Island Grouper with Spiced Rum Beurre Blanc and Pineapple Mango Relish

Chèvre Cheesecake

Cuban Black Bean Soup

Cover the beans with water and soak for 12 hours or overnight.

Drain the beans and place them in a pot with 2 qts. cold water. Simmer for about 1½ hours over low heat. Skim off the scum from the top of the beans as needed.

Sauté the bacon, onion and garlic together and add to the beans. Add the potato, ham, cumin, thyme and bay leaf. Add water until beans are covered. Simmer for 45 minutes.

Remove the bay leaf and season to taste. Divide into soup bowls and sprinkle with onions, rice and parsley.

Serves 8
Preparation Time:
  2¼ Hours
(note soaking time)

  2 cups black beans
  ¼ cup bacon, diced
  1 large onion, chopped
    (reserve ¼ cup for
    garnish)
  1 clove garlic, crushed
  1 large potato, peeled,
    diced
  ¼ cup ham, diced
  ½ tsp. cumin
  ½ tsp. thyme
  1 small bay leaf
    Salt and pepper to
    taste
  ¼ cup cooked rice, for
    garnish
  1 Tbsp. parsley, chopped,
    for garnish

★

Green Salad with Orange Vinaigrette

Serves 8
Preparation Time:
  10 Minutes

  6 Tbsps. red wine
     vinegar
  2 Tbsps. soy sauce
  4 Tbsps. orange juice
  ¾ cup salad oil
  ½ tsp. shallots, chopped
     fine
  ¼ tsp. red pepper flakes
  1 small clove garlic,
     crushed
  ½ tsp. salt
  ½ tsp. black pepper
  2 heads Romaine
     lettuce, torn, rinsed,
     patted dry
  ¾ cup Swiss cheese,
     shredded
  3 Tbsps. sesame seeds

ombine the vinegar, soy sauce, orange juice, oil, shallots, red pepper flakes, garlic, salt and pepper in a bowl, mixing well.

In a separate bowl, combine the lettuce with half the cheese and half the sesame seeds. Pour the dressing over the salad and toss gently.

Arrange on 8 serving plates and sprinkle with the remaining cheese and sesame seeds.

☆

Island Grouper with Spiced Rum Beurre Blanc and Pineapple-Mango Relish

I n a large mixing bowl, combine the pineapple, mango, bell pepper, chile, cilantro, vinegar, lemon juice, oil and salt and pepper. Let flavors blend for 1 hour in the refrigerator.

Cut the grouper filets into eight 6-oz. pieces. Set aside.

In a mixing bowl, combine the macadamia nuts with the bread crumbs.

Coat the grouper filets with the flour. Dip them in the eggs, allowing the excess to drain off. Then coat them with the bread crumb-nut mixture.

Sauté the filets in butter until they are cooked through and golden brown on both sides.

To serve, cover the fish with the warm beurre blanc. Place some of the fruit relish next to the filet.

Serves 8
Preparation Time:
  30 Minutes
(note marinating time)

Pineapple-Mango Relish:

$\frac{2}{3}$ cup fresh pineapple, peeled, diced
$\frac{2}{3}$ cup fresh mango, peeled, diced
$\frac{1}{3}$ cup red bell pepper, stemmed, seeded, diced
  1 small serrano chile, stemmed, seeded, diced
  2 Tbsps. fresh cilantro leaves, chopped
$\frac{1}{3}$ cup rice vinegar
  1 Tbsp. lemon juice
$\frac{1}{3}$ cup olive oil
  Salt and pepper to taste

Grouper:

  3 lbs. grouper filets, boneless, skinless
$1\frac{1}{2}$ cups macadamia nuts, ground
$1\frac{1}{2}$ cups bread crumbs
  2 cups flour
  4 eggs, lightly beaten
  8 oz. butter (2 sticks)
  Spiced rum beurre blanc (recipe follows)

☆

Spiced Rum Beurre Blanc

Preparation Time:
5 Minutes

2 Tbsps. shallots,
chopped fine

2 Tbsps. rice vinegar

4 Tbsps. spiced rum

4 Tbsps. heavy cream

8 oz. butter (2 sticks),
cold, cubed
Salt and pepper to
taste

n a small saucepan, combine the shallots and vinegar. Boil slowly until almost all the liquid is gone. Add the rum and reduce by half.

Add the cream and again reduce by half. Using a small wire whisk, beat while gradually adding the butter, cube by cube. Reduce the heat halfway through. When the last butter cube beaten in, the sauce should be warm rather than hot. Season to taste.

★

Chèvre Cheesecake

n a food processor, beat together the goat cheese and cream cheese, sugar and cream. Add the eggs and vanilla extract.

Butter and sugar-coat eight 4-oz. timbales and fill with the cream mixture.

Bake for approximately 1 hour at 275°. Check with a toothpick to test for doneness. Chill.

Unmold and cover the sides with the chopped hazelnuts.

Serves 8
Preparation Time:
  20 Minutes
Preheat oven to 275°

  ¾ lb. goat cheese
  ½ lb. cream cheese
  ½ cup sugar
  ⅛ cup heavy cream
  4 eggs
  1 Tbsp. vanilla extract
  ⅓ cup hazelnuts, toasted, chopped

CHEZ PIERRE

FRENCH CUISINE
1215 Thomasville Road
Tallahassee, Florida 32303
(850) 222-0936
Lunch Monday–Saturday 11AM–2:30PM
Dinner Monday–Saturday 5:30PM–10PM
Average Dinner for Two: $60

Located in an exquisitely restored 1920s vintage villa, Chez Pierre will charm diners with its breezy decks, front porch and cozy porches. With the philosophy of serving "Traditional French Cuisine with Southern Hospitality," it does not need any explanation.

A restaurant of this class depends on strong talent and heavy experience. Proprietors Eric Favier and Karen Cooley—attractive partners in both business and marriage—fill the bill. Born, reared and trained in the south of France, he is a multi-dimensional chef and pâtissier. Her vitae includes the general management of country clubs and steak-and-ale restaurants. Together they have successfully piloted Chez Pierre for six years.

If sauces are the measure of the cook, these cooks shine. Fresh fish are showcased in a robust reduction of red wine, thyme, veal stock and chicken juices. A saffron wine sauce enhances fresh salmon, the black-olive sauce finishes freshly grilled poultry. Chez Pierre's fabled pastry tray is filled with tempting goodies such as berry-topped Rhum Babas, Mousses, Cookies, Creams and Cakes. It is irresistible.

CHEZ PIERRE'S MENU FOR SIX:

Marinated Lamb

Onion Gratin

Red Wine Poached Pears

Marinated Lamb

P lace lamb, carrots, onions and olive oil in a large mixing bowl. Mix lightly with rosemary, thyme, bay leaves, orange rind, salt and pepper and place in refrigerator overnight.

In a small bowl, place the white beans in water and let soak overnight.

The next day, cook the white beans until tender. Set aside.

Heat 3 Tbsps. of the marinade oil in a heavy-bottomed pan. Add the salt pork, half of the carrots and onions from the marinade, the garlic and the lamb. Mix again with salt and pepper and cover with the rest of the carrots and onions. Add the wine.

Reduce the heat and cover. Cook on low heat for 2 hours or until tender. Remove the bay leaves and orange rind. Add the beans and check seasoning.

Serve in a shallow serving dish sprinkled with parsley.

Serves 6
Preparation Time:
 2½ Hours
(note marinating and
 soaking times)

4 lbs. lamb shoulder, cut
 into 2-inch cubes
3 carrots, thickly sliced
3 onions, chopped
5 Tbsps. olive oil
1 Tbsp. rosemary
2 tsps. thyme
2 bay leaves
3 orange rind pieces,
 2 inches each
1 tsp. salt
1 tsp. black pepper
1 cup white beans, dried
⅓ cup lean salt pork,
 chopped
3 cloves garlic, chopped
2 cups dry white wine
2 Tbsps. parsley,
 chopped

☆

Onion Gratin

Serves 8
Preparation Time:
  40 Minutes
Preheat oven to 350°

  4 lbs. onions
  5 Tbsps. butter
  2 Tbsps. olive oil
    Salt and black pepper
    to taste
    Nutmeg to taste
  3 Tbsps. heavy cream
  4 Tbsps. Swiss cheese,
    grated
    Fresh thyme for
    garnish

ince the onions coarsely by hand and cook them slowly in 3 Tbsps. butter and the oil on top of the stove for 10 minutes, stirring, until soft.

Add the salt, pepper, nutmeg and cream. Check the seasonings and pour the mixture into a buttered, ovenproof dish.

Sprinkle with cheese, dot with the rest of the butter and bake at 350° for 30 minutes.

Garnish with thyme before serving.

☆

Red Wine Poached Pears

Wash and dry the lemon and orange and peel off only the zesty surface. Then cut the whole orange rind and half of the lemon rind into thin strips. Squeeze the lemon and save the juice.

Simmer the wine, sugar and rind in a heavy pan and leave uncovered for several minutes. Add the pears, cover and simmer for 35 to 45 minutes. Baste the pears and turn gently with a wooden spoon so they cook evenly. Prick with a toothpick to test for doneness. The pears should be soft but not mushy.

Remove them with a spoon and place in a serving dish.

Add the fruit purée or preserves to the wine and simmer 15 minutes. Stir in the lemon juice and pour it over the pears. Garnish with fresh mint.

Cooking Secret: The pears are delicious dusted with sugar and caramelized under the broiler before serving.

Serves 6
Preparation Time:
  1 Hour

  1 lemon
    Rind from 1 orange
  2 **cups strong red wine**
  1 **cup sugar**
  6 **large, ripe pears,**
    peeled, cored
  2 **Tbsps. fresh**
    strawberry, raspberry
    purée or preserves
    Fresh mint sprigs for
    garnish

★

JAMIE'S FRENCH RESTAURANT

FRENCH CUISINE
424 East Zarragossa
Pensacola, Florida 32501
(850) 434-2911
Lunch Tuesday–Saturday 11:30AM–2:30PM
Dinner Monday–Saturday 6PM–10PM
Average Dinner for Two: $65

I nside a framed cottage built before 1884, Jamie's French Restaurant features Provençal-style French cuisine. Classic sauces are intensely rich, with carefully selected flavors, using fresh ingredients and reduced to an essence. Recipient of Florida Trend's "Golden Spoon Top Restaurants" award for the last 10 years and *The Wine Spectator's* "Award of Excellence" since 1992, Gary Serafin, proprietor, prides himself on consistency of quality.

House specialties are the Pepperoni-Wrapped Pork Loin, grilled and served with a Feta Cheese and Sun-Dried Tomato Stuffing. Black Walnut-Crusted Baby Rack of New Zealand Lamb is served in a Port Wine Reduction Sauce with Caramelized Pears. Fresh Sautéed Shrimp and Scallops are infused with Fresh Herbs, Grilled Mushrooms and Tomatoes on Pasta.

JAMIE'S FRENCH RESTAURANT'S MENU FOR FOUR:

Grilled Portobello Mushrooms with Crab Meat and Tarragon Béarnaise Sauce

Chilled Zucchini Soup

Pistachio-Encrusted Tuna with Tropical Fruit Beurre Blanc Sauce

Grilled Portobello Mushrooms with Crab Meat and Tarragon Béarnaise Sauce

For the béarnaise: Mix the shallots, tarragon, ¼ cup white wine and tarragon vinegar together in small saucepan. Reduce until all the liquid is gone. Cool and set aside.

In a separate, stainless steel bowl, mix together the egg yolk, remaining wine, lemon juice, Tabasco Sauce and Worcestershire. Heat the bowl over a pot of boiling water. Cook until the egg yolk thickens, stirring constantly. Do not over-cook. Remove from heat. Add the butter in a slow, steady stream. Fold in the tarragon mixture and set aside.

Blend the mustard, garlic, vinegar and oil and place the mushrooms in this marinade. Place the mushrooms in the marinade for 1 hour. Grill the mushrooms over an open flame for about 2 minutes on each side.

Heat the crab, scallions and salt and pepper in a sauté pan.

Mound a quarter of the crab meat in the center of each serving plate. Slice each mushroom into 5 pieces and arrange around the crab meat. Top with Tarragon Béarnaise and serve.

Serves 4
Preparation Time:
 30 Minutes
(note marinating time)

 1 Tbsp. shallots, chopped
½ cup dried tarragon
¼ cup + 1 Tbsp. white wine
¼ cup tarragon vinegar
 1 egg yolk
 1 Tbsp. lemon juice
 Dash of Tabasco Sauce
 Dash of Worcestershire sauce
½ lb. butter, melted, kept hot
¼ cup Dijon mustard
¼ tsp. garlic, minced
¼ cup balsamic vinegar
 1 cup olive oil
 4 large portobello mushrooms, stemmed
½ lb. crab meat
 1 Tbsp. scallions, chopped
 Salt and pepper to taste

☆

Chilled Zucchini Soup

Serves 4
Preparation Time:
 30 Minutes
(note refrigeration time)

¼ cup olive oil
1 medium onion,
    coarsely chopped
6 to 8 medium zucchini,
    trimmed, scrubbed,
    cut into ¼-inch slices
2 cloves garlic, minced
4 cups heavy cream
    Pinch of thyme
    Salt and pepper to
    taste
    Dill for garnish

eat oil in a large, heavy skillet over medium heat. Add the onion and sauté, stirring occasionally, until the onion is softened.

Add the zucchini and garlic. Reduce heat to low. Cover and simmer until browned. Remove pan from heat. Stir in 2 cups of the heavy cream and the thyme. Let cool slightly.

Place half the zucchini mixture in a blender or food processor. Blend until smooth. Transfer to a large bowl. Stir in ⅓ cup of heavy cream. Repeat the procedure with the remaining zucchini and heavy cream.

Force the soup through a fine sieve. Add salt and pepper to taste.

Refrigerate for several hours before serving.

Garnish soup with dill before serving.

Cooking Secret: If a coarser textured soup is desired, do not put through the sieve.

Pistachio Encrusted Tuna with Tropical Fruit Beurre Blanc Sauce

I n a food processor, combine the pistachios, bread crumbs, curry, garlic and onion powders, salt and pepper.

Set up a breading station with three separate bowls: flour, egg wash made of egg and milk beaten together and nut mixture. Place the tuna in flour, then egg wash, then nut mixture.

Sauté the tuna in 2 Tbsps. olive oil over high heat until brown on both sides. Finish cooking in a 350° oven for approximately 5 minutes.

For the sauce, combine the mango, kiwi, pineapple and Key lime juice. Reserve at room temperature.

In a flat-bottomed saucepan over medium heat, reduce the shallots and wine until almost dry. Remove from heat. Swirl the butter into the mixture until a sauce forms. Fold the fruit into the sauce.

Serve tuna with sauce and fruit drizzled over the top.

Serves 4
Preparation Time:
  35 Minutes
Preheat oven to 350°

  1 cup pistachios
  1 cup bread crumbs
  1 tsp. curry powder
  ½ tsp. powdered garlic
  ½ tsp. powdered onion
  ½ tsp. salt
  ½ tsp. black pepper
  1 cup flour
  1 egg, beaten
  1 cup milk
  4 tuna steaks, 6 oz. each
  2 Tbsps. olive oil
  ½ cup mango, diced
  ¼ cup kiwi, diced
  ¼ cup pineapple, diced
  2 Tbsps. Key lime juice
  3 Tbsps. shallots, chopped
  ½ cup white wine
  ½ lb. butter, cut into small pieces, at room temperature

★

SOVEREIGN

CONTINENTAL CUISINE
12 Southeast Second Avenue
Gainesville, Florida 32601
(352) 378-6307
Dinner Monday–Friday 5:30PM–10PM
Dinner Saturday 5:30PM–11PM
Average Dinner for Two: $60

Comfortably housed in a historically restored 19th century carriage house, the Sovereign has been an innovative leader in fine Florida dining since its opening in 1976. Stained-glass windows serve as dividers between former horse stalls. From the crystal to the candlelight to the jazz pianist, the Sovereign has been noted for its ambiance, cuisine and history.

Their recipe for success is simple and undeviating. Chef/owner Elmo Moser prepares each menu item using the freshest ingredients. And the kitchen and service staff are trained as coordinated units, providing quality service and attention to the smallest details.

Menu highlights include Breast of Chicken and Green Noodles Sautéed with Blackberry Vinegar, Rack of Lamb in a Tomato and Honey Mint Sauce and Butterflied Prawns Marinated in Herbs and Olive Oil. Be sure to see the dessert menu.

SOVEREIGN'S MENU FOR FOUR:

Shrimp à la Cove

Potato and Leek Soup

Drunken Fish Casserole

Shrimp à la Cove

S eason the flour with salt and pepper. Dust the shrimp in flour, shaking off any excess.

Heat the oil in a sauté pan over medium heat.

Add the shrimp and garlic, tossing constantly. When shrimp turns pink and feels firm, pour in the wine and lemon juice.

Add the onions.

Serve immediately.

Serves 4
Preparation Time:
  10 Minutes

¼ **cup flour**
  Salt and pepper to taste
24 **large shrimps, peeled, deveined**
 3 **Tbsps. olive oil**
 1 **tsp. garlic, finely chopped**
 2 **Tbsps. white wine**
 2 **Tbsps. fresh lemon juice**
 4 **Tbsps. green onions, chopped**

☆

Potato and Leek Soup

Serves 4
Preparation Time:
50 Minutes

3 Tbsps. oil
3 thick leeks, white part
   only, chopped
1 medium onion,
   chopped
2 large potatoes, peeled,
   cubed
4 Tbsps. flour
8 cups chicken stock
   Salt and white pepper
   to taste
¼ cup water
½ tsp. oregano
1 cup heavy cream

n a large, heavy pot, heat the oil and sauté the leeks until soft.

Add the onion, potatoes and 2 Tbsps. flour and mix well.

Add the stock. Season with salt and pepper. Bring to a boil, then turn heat down and cook 15 minutes uncovered. Reduce the heat.

In a small bowl mix together the remaining 2 Tbsps. flour and water. Slowly add the flour mixture to the soup, stirring as it thickens.

Add oregano and cream. Adjust the seasonings to taste

Drunken Fish Casserole

I n a large, deep skillet, put the butter and garlic and sauté lightly until the garlic is translucent.

Add the tomatoes and clam juice.

Turn up the heat and add the lobster tails, clams and fish filets. Bring to a boil for about 2 minutes.

Add the remaining seafood and season with salt and pepper.

Add the bourbon, reduce heat and cover with a lid. Cook for 1 to 2 minutes or until seafood is cooked through.

Serve in large, deep bowls over rice.

Serves 4
Preparation Time:
  30 Minutes

  2 Tbsps. butter
  2 tsps. garlic, chopped
  2 tomatoes, peeled,
    seeded, chopped
  4 cups clam juice
  2 lobster tails, cut in half
    vertically, shell on
 12 clams
  4 grouper filets, 4 oz.
    each
 12 large shrimp, peeled,
    deveined, tails left on
 12 medium scallops
  8 oysters
    Salt and black pepper
    to taste
  4 Tbsps. bourbon
  2 cups white rice,
    cooked

☆

TOP OF DAYTONA

FRENCH AND ITALIAN CUISINE
2625 South Atlantic Avenue
Daytona Beach Shores, Florida 32118
(904) 767-5791
Open Daily Lunch and Dinner
Average Dinner for Two: $45

 ocated on the 29th floor of the tallest oceanfront building on the Atlantic Coast, Top of Daytona offers magnificent panoramic views from every seat in the elegant dining room.

A unique menu features a combination of Italian, French and American entrées, a great selection of appetizers and house-made desserts. In fact, all of the dressings, cheese, gravlox and desserts are made in-house.

The executive chef, Vadim Vladimirsky, a New York French culinary school graduate, was trained by world-famous chefs like Jacques Pepin and Adre Saltner.

A comfortable and spacious bar lounge is complimented by live entertainment and a dance floor.

TOP OF DAYTONA MENU FOR TWO:

Grilled Pork Tenderloin with Beet Vinaigrette

Chicken Scarpedella

Tiramisu

Grilled Pork Tenderloin with Beet Vinaigrette

Marinate the pork tenderloin with 1 cup olive oil, thyme and steak seasoning. Refrigerate it for 2 hours.

For the vinaigrette: Steam the beets until cooked through, remove from heat and chill. Peel the beet and place it in a food processor with the shallot, garlic, Dijon mustard and red wine vinegar. Process the mixture for 1 minute and add 1 cup olive oil, slowly. Strain and season with salt and pepper to taste.

Remove the pork from the marinade and grill it until the tenderloin reaches an internal temperature of 155° or until it is just barely pink at the center; do not overcook.

To serve, pool the sauce in the middle of each serving plate and place pork cut into ¼-inch slices on the top. Garnish with chopped parsley.

Serves 2
Preparation Time:
  45 Minutes
(note marinating time)

- 1 lb. pork tenderloin
- 2 cups olive oil
  Sprig of thyme, roughly chopped
- 1 cup of steak seasoning of your choice
- 2 large beets
- 1 shallot
- 3 garlic cloves
- 1 Tbsp. Dijon mustard
- ⅓ cup red wine vinegar
  Salt and pepper to taste
  Parsley, chopped for garnish

☆

Chicken Scarpedella

Serves 2
Preparation Time:
30 Minutes

2 chicken breasts
¼ cup olive oil
1 shallot, chopped
2 Tbsps. garlic, chopped
Pinch of crushed
pepper
⅓ lb. sweet Italian
sausage, sliced
⅓ lb. shiitake
mushrooms, sliced
1 sprig of fresh rosemary
¼ cup chicken stock
5 Tbsps. white wine
¼ cup balsamic vinegar
2 Tbsps. unsalted butter
Salt and pepper to
taste
Rosemary for garnish

R inse chicken breasts and slice into ½-inch slices.
In a large skillet, heat the olive oil over medium-high heat. Brown the chicken on all sides, about 5 minutes altogether.

Add the shallot, garlic, crushed pepper, sausage, mushrooms and rosemary. Sauté for 1 to 2 minutes.

Add the chicken stock, wine and vinegar. Lower heat and reduce liquid by ¾. Remove from heat.

Remove chicken from skillet and place on a serving plate.

Swirl butter into the reduced sauce off the stove and pour it over the chicken.

Garnish with a sprig of fresh rosemary.

Tiramisu

Brew 3 cups of espresso and set aside until it is just warm.

In a mixing bowl, add the mascarpone cheese, sugar, egg yolks, Marsala wine, brandy and butterscotch schnapps. Blend thoroughly until mixture becomes very heavy, then set aside.

Dip lady fingers in warm espresso for approximately 2 seconds, one at a time. Lay them side by side, row by row, in a 2-inch deep sheet pan until the bottom and sides are covered.

Next add ½ of the mascarpone mixture and evenly layer the top of the lady fingers. Repeat these layers until last layer is lady fingers.

Powder top of dessert with cocoa powder.

Chill approximately 1 hour before serving. Then slice into four equal servings and serve.

Cooking Secret: This recipe can easily serve either eight people or four very hungry ones!

Serves 4
Preparation Time:
  30 Minutes
(note refrigeration time)

  3 cups Italian espresso
  1 lb. mascarpone cheese
  ⅓ cup granulated sugar
  2 egg yolks
  1 tsp. dry red Marsala wine
  1 tsp. brandy
  2 tsps. butterscotch schnapps
  3 dozen lady fingers
  2 to 3 Tbsps. cocoa powder

☆

CASA DE LA PAZ

22 Avenida Menendez
St. Augustine, Florida 32084
(800) 939-2915
(904) 829-2915
Web Page: www.oldcity.com/delapaz
Room Rates: $89–$169

When travelers arrive at the historic Casa de la Paz, they immediately realize they have entered the "House of Peace." Built in 1915, this elegant, Mediterranean-style home offers views of the bay, the historic Bridge of Lions and the lighthouse.

Every room and suite has a private bath, queen-sized, wrought iron bed and a decanter of sherry. With names such as the Ponce de Leon Room and the Marco Polo Room, it is even more tempting to explore the history-rich city of St. Augustine.

Guests awake to the aroma of freshly baked quiches, muffins, cakes and even homemade apple butter. Dining in the sunny conservatory is an extraordinary way to begin your day. In the afternoons you can relax and enjoy a glass of wine in the Spanish courtyard, surrounded by tropical flowers and a fountain.

Chicken Salad with Cranberry Vinaigrette

I n a large bowl combine the chicken, celery, mayonnaise, sour cream, grapes, pecans and salt and pepper. Refrigerate.

Make the vinaigrette in a blender by combining the olive oil, vinegar, salt, sugar, pepper, paprika, mustard and cranberry sauce. Purée until smooth.

Before serving pour the vinaigrette over the chicken salad.

Serves 8 to 10
Preparation Time:
 15 Minutes

 4 cups chicken, cooked, diced
 1 cup celery, chopped
 ½ cup mayonnaise
 ½ cup sour cream
 2 cups white seedless grapes
 ½ cup salted pecans, toasted, chopped
 Salt and pepper to taste
 ¾ cup olive oil
 ¼ cup red wine vinegar
 1 tsp. salt
 1 tsp. sugar
 ½ tsp. pepper
 ½ tsp. paprika
 ¼ tsp. dry mustard
 ½ cup whole cranberry sauce

☆

Casa de Solana
Bed and Breakfast Inn

21 Aviles Street
St. Augustine, Florida 32084
(800) 760-3556
(904) 824-3555
Web Page: www.oldcity.com/solana
Room rates: $125–$145

Built in 1763 by a Spanish military officer, Casa de Solana Bed and Breakfast Inn is a renovated colonial home located in the heart of St. Augustine's historic area.

The inn offers four antique-filled guest suites with chocolates, crystal decanters filled with sherry and breathtaking views of Matanzas Bay. By opening the balcony doors you can hear the echo of horses hoofs on brick from the narrow street below. Each morning, guests sit down at the table to a complimentary breakfast of eggs, grits, fresh fruit and home-baked breads.

From Casa de Solana, you can walk to just about all of the historic attractions, fine restaurants, museums and quaint shops.

Tomato and Spring Onion Quiche

Spread the sliced onions over the pie crust. Top with crumbled bacon, green pepper and cheese.

Place the eggs, half and half, salt, pepper and garlic powder in a blender. Blend until well mixed. Pour the egg mixture over the ingredients in the pie crust. Carefully arrange tomato slices on top and sprinkle with Italian seasoning.

Bake at 350° for 30 to 40 minutes.

Serves 6
Preparation Time:
 45 Minutes
Preheat oven to 350°

 1 pastry shell, 9 inches
 1 cup green onions,
   sliced
 4 bacon strips, cooked
   crispy, crumbled
 1 green pepper, diced
   (optional)
 1 cup cheddar cheese,
   grated
 5 eggs
 ¾ cup half and half
   Salt and black pepper
   to taste
 ⅛ tsp. garlic powder
 3 to 4 plum tomatoes,
   thickly sliced
 1 tsp. Italian seasoning

☆

CEDAR HOUSE INN

79 Cedar Street
St. Augustine, Florida 32084
(800) CEDAR INN
(904) 829-0079
Room Rates: $64–$150

The Cedar House Inn, a restored Victorian home built in 1893, is located in a quiet residential neighborhood in the heart of the historic city. Although the inn is "off the beaten track," it is within walking distance of all the major historic sites, antique shops, art galleries and restaurants.

Guests can relax on the shady wraparound porch or in the grand parlor with its fireplace, player piano and antique Victrola. Each themed bedroom has a balcony with a private entrance, queen-sized bed and private bathroom. Some of the rooms have turn-of-the-century claw-footed tubs, while others have Jacuzzis.

Other features of the inn include an outside Jacuzzi spa in the garden gazebo and bicycles that guests can use to explore the city. An elegant, complimentary full breakfast, which is gaining a reputation as a gourmet's delight, is served each morning.

Minorcan Egg Cups

Spray the inside of 6 muffin cups and press a tortilla into each cup. Make sure the tortilla covers the entire inside. Cut off and discard the overlap.

In a large mixing bowl, beat the eggs with the milk. Add the cheese, salt, pepper and hot sauce.

Pour egg mixture into the muffin cups and fold in 1 Tbsp. of corn and ¼ tsp. green onions per cup.

Cook in a 350° oven for 20 minutes or until the eggs are set and the tops are lightly browned.

Serve with tomatoes, sour cream and salsa.

Cooking Secret: Minorcan refers to a variety of spicy St. Augustine food whose heritage is traced to early pioneers from the Island of Minorca, which lies in the Mediterranean Sea off the coast of Spain.

Serves 6
Preparation Time:
  25 Minutes
Preheat oven to 350°

  6 white corn tortillas,
    6-inch
  6 eggs
  6 Tbsps. low fat milk
  6 Tbsps. cheddar cheese,
    shredded
    Salt and pepper to
    taste
  6 dashes of hot sauce
  1 small can whole kernel
    corn
  2 green onions, chopped
  2 small tomatoes, sliced
  6 Tbsps. sour cream
    Chunky salsa

☆

DAYTONA BEACH HILTON OCEANFRONT RESORT

2637 South Atlantic Avenue
Daytona Beach, Florida 32118
(800) 221-2424
(904) 767-7350
Room Rates: $79–$164

This 11-story hotel overlooks the beach, with spectacular views of the Atlantic Ocean or Intracoastal Waterway. Recently renovated, the island-style decor is matched by top-notch resort services and amenities. Breezy tropical colors, natural wood trim, rattan furniture and cool tile accents provide an exquisite backdrop to the oceanfront setting.

Spacious, comfortable guest rooms contain a wet bar and mini-refrigerator as well as private terraces or balconies. From morning coffee on the balcony to dinner and a movie in your room, room service is yours to enjoy any time of day.

The Blue Water Grille highlights Mediterranean and Caribbean cuisine. On weekend nights the Blue Water Lounge features piano music.

Blackened Chicken Tortellini

Coat the chicken with the seasoning and black in a sauté pan until fully done. Cool, then dice.

Blanch the tortellini in salted, boiling water and drain.

In a sauté pan, sauté the vegetables and garlic in olive oil until lightly browned over medium heat. Deglaze with chicken stock and add the heavy cream.

Add the tortellini. Toss together and reduce over low heat.

Salt and pepper to taste.

Add the diced chicken and toss in a serving bowl.

Top with grated Parmesan cheese.

Serves 2
Preparation Time:
 20 Minutes

- 2 chicken breasts, 6 oz. each
  Blackening seasoning to taste
- ½ lb. spinach tortellini
- 1 red pepper, julienne
- ½ cup broccoli florets
- ½ red onion, julienne
- 4 cloves garlic, sliced
- 2 Tbsps. olive oil
- ½ cup chicken broth
- ¼ cup heavy cream
  Salt and pepper to taste
  Parmesan cheese, grated, to taste

HERLONG MANSION

402 Cholokka Boulevard
P.O. Box 667
Micanopy, Florida 32667
(800) HERLONG
(352) 466-3322
Room Rates: $55–$165

Set back from the street and surrounded by lovely gardens, this tastefully appointed Southern mansion embodies romantic ambiance. All the rooms and suites are unique in their furnishings and character.

Among the architectural highlights are the leaded-glass windows, ten fireplaces, inlaid mahogany, maple and oak floors, twelve-foot ceilings and floor-to-ceiling windows.

In the morning, guests awaken to homemade pastries, croissants, eggs, sausage, fresh fruit, tea and coffee. The Herlong Mansion is an oasis from the hustle and bustle of everyday life, yet only minutes from shopping, theaters and many fine restaurants.

Hash Brown Quiche

Grease a large-sized muffin pan. Press the hash browns down into the muffin cups to form a crust. Brush or drizzle with melted butter.

Bake 25 to 30 minutes at 425°. Reduce oven temperature to 350°.

Fill crusts with cheese.

In a mixing bowl, whisk together the milk, eggs, cayenne pepper and garlic salt. Pour into the muffin cups and bake for 30 to 40 minutes or until a toothpick inserted into the center comes out clean.

Allow to cool before removing from pan.

Serves 6
Preparation Time:
  1 Hour
Preheat oven to 425°

10 oz. hash browns, shredded, refrigerated or frozen
2½ Tbsps. butter, melted
2 cups mild cheddar cheese, shredded
3 cups milk
6 eggs
   Cayenne pepper to taste
   Garlic salt to taste

☆

HOYT HOUSE BED AND BREAKFAST

804 Atlantic Avenue
Amelia Island, Florida 32034
(800) 432-2085
(904) 277-4300
Web Page: www.hoythouse.com
E-mail: hoythouse@net-magic.net
Room Rates: $80–$139

Stroll up the brick path and enter through the double "Yankee doors" into a home that was built when charm and elegance abounded. Like the warmth of a winter fire, Hoyt House draws all who visit into a warm embrace. It's a beautiful example of Victorian architecture in the Queen Anne style.

The romantic atmosphere is found throughout the bed and breakfast. Couples often exchange vows beneath the garlanded gazebo or within the Victorian mansion.

The ambiance of each room is unique, with a style of its own. Antique furnishings, custom window treatments and inspired color schemes combine to encompass you in its warmth. The Desert Sunset Room features a queen-sized, sleigh bed. The largest and grandest of the nine rooms is the Sweet Lavender Room. In addition to its beautiful view of St. Peter Church, the room features a queen-sized, four-poster rice bed, fireplace and separate dressing area. All the rooms have private baths.

In the morning, guests enjoy a homemade breakfast before going off to explore Amelia Island.

Omelet Sandwich

C oat two 13×9×2-inch baking dishes with non stick spray. Line dish with half the bread slices which that have been cut to fit the casseroles. Arrange cheese and ham on the bread slices on top like a sandwich. Set aside.

Combine eggs, milk, salt and dry mustard. Mix well and pour over bread. Cover and refrigerate overnight.

In the morning, remove from refrigerator and let stand for 30 minutes. Sprinkle with corn flakes. Drizzle butter over the top.

Bake in oven for 45 to 50 minutes. Let stand for 5 minutes before cutting.

Serves 10
Preparation Time:
 40 Minutes
(note refrigeration time)
Preheat oven to 325°

16 white bread slices,
  crusts removed
8 American cheese slices
8 ham slices, cut into
  1-inch strips
6 eggs, beaten
3 cups milk
½ tsp. salt
½ tsp. dry mustard
1 cup corn flakes,
  crushed
2 Tbsps. butter, melted

ISLAND HOTEL

P.O. Box 460
Cedar Key, Florida 32625
(352) 543-5111
Web Page: www.gnv.fdt.net/~ishotel/
E-mail: ishotel@gnv.fdt.net
Room Rates: $85–$95

Listed on the National Register of Historic Buildings, this charming inn is one of Florida's most famous bed and breakfasts. Built in 1859, the Island Hotel has withstood hurricanes and the passage of time for more than 125 years.

Guests are encouraged to relax in a rocker on the balcony and watch the sunset over the Gulf.

The Island Hotel has 13 guest rooms. To preserve the romantic and traditional ambiance, there are no telephones or televisions in the guest rooms. Some have old fashioned claw-foot tubs and all have the original hand-hewn wooden walls and floors.

The restaurant features gourmet cuisine utilizing the region's bounty, including soft-shell crabs, oysters and stone crabs.

Palm Salad

 n a large bowl, blend the first 4 ingredients until smooth. Freeze to ice cream consistency, or approximately 4 hours.

In two shallow salad dishes arrange the lettuce. Cover the base with a layer of palm cabbage. Decorate with fruit to taste. Sprinkle with dates.

Place one large scoop of ice cream mixture in the center of the salad base and serve immediately.

Serves 2
Preparation Time:
  5 Minutes
(note freezing time)

  1 **pint vanilla ice cream**
  1 **pint lime sherbet**
 ¼ **cup crunchy peanut**
    butter
 ¼ **cup mayonnaise**
    Lettuce
 ½ **cup fresh or canned**
    hearts of palm
 ½ **cup fresh fruit (e.g.**
    bananas, berries,
    melon, kiwi,
    pineapple, etc.)
  1 **Tbsp. dates, chopped**

KENWOOD INN

38 Marine Street
St. Augustine, Florida 32084
(904) 824-2116
Web Page: www.travelbase.com/destinations/st-augustine/kenwood
Room Rates: $85–$150

Since 1886, the Kenwood Inn has been providing a friendly haven for visitors to St. Augustine. This lovely Victorian building has maintained the charm and character of its 100 years of tradition, while now providing a casual, elegant style.

With accommodations ranging from one room to a three-room bridal suite with water views, there is something for everyone.

Homemade cakes, breads, muffins, fruit juices and coffee tempt guests out of their comfortable rooms. Visitors to the inn gather each morning in the dining room and enjoy good food and good conversation with other guests.

The walled courtyard is the perfect place to sit and relax after a long day of sightseeing. On hot and humid days, guests cool off in the refreshing pool.

Pumpkin Bread

In a medium-sized bowl, mix together dry ingredients.
 In a separate bowl, mix together the oil and water.
Make a well in the dry ingredients. Add the oil-water mixture, beaten eggs, pumpkin and mix well. Fold in nuts. Pour into greased loaf pans.
 Bake at 350° for 1 hour.

Yield: 2 loaves
Preparation Time:
 10 Minutes
Preheat oven to 350°

3½ cups flour
 3 cups sugar
 2 tsps. baking soda
1½ tsps. salt
1½ tsps. cinnamon
 1 tsp. nutmeg
 1 cup oil
 ⅔ cup cold water
 4 eggs, beaten
 1 cup cooked or canned
   pumpkin
 2 cups walnuts, chopped

★

MAGNOLIA PLANTATION

309 Southeast Seventh Street
Gainesville, Florida 32601
(800) 201-2379
(352) 375-6653
Room Rates: $75–$100

T he Magnolia Plantation, named for the many magnolias that surround the house, has been a labor of love for owners Joe and Cindy Montalto. One of the magnolia trees was a gift from Joe's parents, transplanted from Palm Bay to Gainesville in 1980. The inn is decorated with family heirlooms belonging to Cindy's grandparents, who were born in England during the Victorian era.

When guests enter the inn, they are greeted by an impressive 12-foot-wide central hallway with mahogany staircase. The Gentlemen's Parlor and Ladies' Parlor are two of the favorite gathering spots for guests.

The Heather Room, with its ornate white iron queen-sized bed, is adorned with pink lilac accents and has a grand view of the gardens. The Gardenia Room has an 1880s Eastlake Victorian double bed, with a feather mattress placed on top of the regular mattress, for maximum comfort.

In the morning, enjoy a full breakfast in the dining room or on the front or back verandah.

Stuffed French Toast

In a small bowl, combine cream cheese, orange marmalade and honey and stir gently until just combined. In a medium-sized bowl, whisk together the eggs and orange juice.

Spread each slice of bread with the cream cheese mixture and top with another slice of bread. Dip the "sandwiches" in the egg mixture and place in a large, lightly buttered frying pan. Cook until browned on both sides.

Cut into triangles and sprinkle with the sugar. Serve immediately with the orange slices.

Serves 6
Preparation Time:
  25 Minutes

 ¾ **cup cream cheese, softened**
 ⅔ **cup orange marmalade**
 2 **Tbsps. honey**
 5 **eggs**
 1 **cup fresh orange juice**
 12 **bread slices, slightly frozen**
    Confectioners' sugar for garnish
    Orange slices for garnish

★

Marriott's Bay Point Resort Village

4200 Marriott Drive
Panama City Beach, Florida 32408
(800) 874-7105
(904) 234-3307
Room Rates: $60–$189

Situated on a wildlife sanctuary beside beautiful St. Andrews Bay, Bay Point Resort Village is a fun-filled resort with something for everyone. From browsing the boutiques at Silver Sands, to enjoying a meal with friends and family at one of the four restaurants and lounges, to windsurfing, to golfing on two PGA Championship golf courses, the resort is 1,100 acres of endless choices for enjoyment. Guests are invited to attend the hotel's famous theme parties and beach bashes.

The resort offers designer getaway packages for every occasion, including honeymoon, golfing and family vacations.

Shrimp Bayview

Shell the shrimps and devein. Cut the shrimp down the length of the underside and press each one open. Place in a large baking dish.

Melt half the butter in a small sauté pan and cook the bell pepper to soften, about 3 minutes. Add the green onions and cook two more minutes.

Combine the mixture with the mustard, sherry, Worcestershire sauce, crab meat, bread crumbs, parsley and mayonnaise. Add salt and pepper and enough egg to bind together.

Spoon the stuffing onto the shrimp and sprinkle with Parmesan cheese and paprika. Melt the remaining butter and drizzle over the shrimp. Bake at 350° for about 10 minutes.

Serve immediately.

Serves 4
Preparation Time:
 30 Minutes
Preheat oven to 350°

- 24 large shrimps
- 4 Tbsps. butter
- ½ cup red bell pepper, chopped
- ¼ cup green onions, finely chopped
- ½ tsp. dry mustard
- 2 tsps. dry sherry
- 1 tsp. Worcestershire sauce
- 4 oz. crab meat, cooked
- 6 Tbsps. fresh bread crumbs
- 1 Tbsp. parsley, chopped
- 2 Tbsps. mayonnaise
  Salt and pepper to taste
- 1 egg, beaten
- ¼ cup Parmesan cheese, grated
- ½ tsp. Spanish paprika

☆

Conversion Index

LIQUID MEASURES

1 dash	3 to 6 drops
1 teaspoon (tsp.)	⅓ tablespoon
1 tablespoon (Tbsp.)	3 teaspoons
1 tablespoon	½ fluid ounce
1 fluid ounce	2 tablespoons
1 cup	½ pint
1 cup	16 tablespoons
1 cup	8 fluid ounces
1 pint	2 cups
1 pint	16 fluid ounces

DRY MEASURES

1 pinch	less than ⅛ teaspoon
1 teaspoon	⅓ tablespoon
1 tablespoon	3 teaspoons
¼ cup	4 tablespoons
⅓ cup	5 tablespoons plus 1 teaspoon
½ cup	8 tablespoons
⅔ cup	10 tablespoons plus 2 teaspoons
¾ cup	12 tablespoons
1 cup	16 tablespoons

VEGETABLES AND FRUITS

Apple (1 medium)	1 cup chopped
Avocado (1 medium)	1 cup mashed
Broccoli (1 stalk)	2 cups florets
Cabbage (1 large)	10 cups, chopped
Carrot (1 medium)	½ cup, diced
Celery (3 stalks)	1 cup, diced
Eggplant (1 medium)	4 cups, cubed
Lemon (1 medium)	2 tablespoons juice
Onion (1 medium)	1 cup diced
Orange (1 medium)	½ cup juice
Parsley (1 bunch)	3 cups, chopped
Spinach (fresh), 12 cups, loosely packed	1 cup cooked
Tomato (1 medium)	¾ cup, diced
Zucchini (1 medium)	2 cups, diced

APPROXIMATE EQUIVALENTS

1 stick butter = ½ cup = 8 Tbsps. = 4 oz.
1 cup all-purpose flour = 5 oz.
1 cup cornmeal (polenta) = 4½ oz.
1 cup sugar = 8 oz.
1 cup powdered sugar = 4½ oz.
1 cup brown sugar = 6 oz.
1 large egg = 2 oz. = ¼ cup = 4 Tbsps.
1 egg yolk = 1 Tbsp. + 1 tsp.
1 egg white = 2 Tbsps. + 2 tsps.

Metric Conversions

OUNCES TO GRAMS

To convert ounces to grams, multiply number of ounces by 28.35

1 oz. ....30 g.	6 oz. ....180 g.	11 oz........300 g.	16 oz. ......450 g.
2 oz. ....60 g.	7 oz. ....200 g.	12 oz. ......340 g.	20 oz. ......570 g.
3 oz. ....85 g.	8 oz. ....225 g.	13 oz........370 g.	24 oz. ......680 g.
4 oz..........115 g.	9 oz. ....250 g.	14 oz. ......400 g.	28 oz. ......790 g.
5 oz. ....140 g.	10 oz. ......285 g.	15 oz. ......425 g.	32 oz. ......900 g.

QUARTS TO LITERS

To convert quarts to liters, multiply number of quarts by 0.95

1 qt. ....1 L	2½ qt........2½ L	5 qt. ....4¾ L	8 qt...........7½ L
1½ qt. ......1½ L	3 qt. ....2¾ L	6 qt...........5½ L	9 qt...........8½ L
2 qt. ....2 L	4 qt. ....3¾ L	7 qt...........6½ L	10 qt.........9½ L

FAHRENHEIT TO CELSIUS

To convert Fahrenheit to Celsius, subtract 32 from the Fahrenheit figure, multiply by 5, then divide by 9

OTHER METRIC CONVERSIONS

To convert **ounces to milliliters,** multiply number of ounces by 30

To convert **cups to liters,** multiply number of cups by 0.24

To convert **inches to centimeters,** multiply number of inches by 2.54

Glossary of Ingredients

ACHIOTE: a spice blend made from ground annatto seeds, garlic, cumin, vinegar and other spices.

ACORN SQUASH: a oval-shaped winter squash with a ribbed, dark-green skin and orange flesh.

ANAHEIM CHILE: elongated and cone-shaped chiles that are red or green with a mild flavor.

ANCHO CHILE: a shiny-skinned red or green cone-shaped chile with medium heat.

ARBORIO RICE: a large-grained plump rice which requires more cooking time than other rice varieties. Arborio is traditionally used for risotto because its increased starches lend this classic dish its creamy texture.

ARMENIAN CUCUMBER: a long, pale, green-ridged cucumber with an edible skin, also known as the English cucumber.

ARUGULA: also known as rocket or roquette, noted for its strong peppery taste. Arugula makes a lively addition to salads, soups and sautéed vegetable dishes. It's a rich source of iron as well as vitamins A and C.

ASIAN NOODLES: though some Asian-style noodles are wheat-based, many others are made from ingredients such as potato flour, rice flour, buckwheat flour and yam or soybean starch.

BALSAMIC VINEGAR: made from the juice of Trebbiano grapes and traditionally aged in barrels, this tart, sweet, rich vinegar is a versatile ingredient.

BARTLETT PEAR: this large, sweet, bell-shaped fruit has a smooth, yellow-green skin that is sometimes blushed with red.

BASMATI RICE: translated as "queen of fragrance," basmati is a long-grained rice with a nut-like flavor and fine texture.

BÉCHAMEL SAUCE: a basic French white sauce made by stirring milk into a butter-flour roux. Béchamel, the base of many other sauces, was named after its inventor, Louis XIV's steward Louis de Béchamel.

BELGIAN ENDIVE: a white, yellow-edged bitter lettuce that is crunchy.

BLOOD ORANGE: a sweet-tart, thin-skinned orange with a bright red flesh.

BOK CHOY: resembles Swiss chard with its long, thick-stemmed, light green stalks. The flavor is much like cabbage.

BOUQUET GARNI: a group of herbs, such as parsley, thyme and bay leaf, that are placed in a cheesecloth bag and tied together for the use of flavor in soups, stews and broths.

BULGAR WHEAT: wheat kernels that have been steamed, dried and crushed, offering a chewy texture.

CAPERS: available in the gourmet food sections of supermarkets, capers are a small, green, pickled bud of a Mediterranean flowering plant; usually packed in brine.

CARDAMOM: a sweetly pungent, aromatic cooking spice that is a member of the ginger family.

CHANTERELLE MUSHROOM: a trumpet-shaped mushroom that resembles an umbrella turned inside out. One of the more delicious wild mushrooms.

CHÈVRE: cheese made from goat's milk is lower in fat and offers a delicate, light and slightly earthy flavor.

CHICKPEAS: also called garbanzo beans, they have a firm texture and mild, nut-like flavor. Available canned, dried or fresh.

CHICORY or CURLY ENDIVE: a crisp, curly, green-leafed lettuce. Best when young. Tend to bitter with age.

CHILE OIL: a red oil available in Asian stores. Chile oil is also easily made at home by heating 1 cup of vegetable or peanut oil with 2 dozen small dried red chiles or 1 Tbsp. cayenne.

CHIPOTLE PEPPERS: ripened and smoky-flavored jalapeño peppers have a fiery heat and delicious flavor.

CHOW-CHOW: a mustard-flavored mixed vegetable and pickle relish.

CLARIFIED BUTTER: also called drawn butter. This is an unsalted butter that has been slowly melted, thereby evaporating most of the water and separating the milk solids, which sink to the bottom of the pan. After any foam is skimmed off the top, the clear butter is poured off the milk residue and used in cooking.

COCONUT MILK: available in Asian markets, this milk is noted for its richly flavored, slightly sweet taste. Coconut milk can be made by placing 2 cups of finely grated chopped fresh coconut in 3 cups scalded milk. Stir and let stand until the milk cools to room temperature. Strain before using.

COULIS: a general term referring to a thick purée or sauce.

COURT BOUILLON: a broth made by cooking various vegetables and herbs in water.

CRÈME FRAÎCHE: a bit richer than sour cream, yet more tart than whipped heavy cream. It can be purchased in most supermarkets or made by whisking together ½ cup heavy or whipping cream, not ultra-pasteurized, with ½ cup sour cream. Pour the mixture into a jar, cover and let stand in a warm, dark area for 24 hours. This will yield 1 cup which can be kept in the refrigerator for about 10 days.

CRESS: resembles radish leaves, with a hot peppery flavor.

DATIL PEPPERS: type of small yellow hot peppers that grow in the Saint Augustine area. They are similar to a jalapeño pepper but have their own distinctive flavor and "heat".

EGGPLANT: commonly thought of as a vegetable, eggplant is actually a fruit. The very narrow, straight Japanese or Oriental eggplant has a tender, slightly sweet flesh. The Italian or baby eggplant looks like a miniature version of the common large variety, but has a more delicate skin and flesh. The egg-shaped white eggplant makes the name of this fruit understandable.

FAVA BEANS: tan flat beans that resemble very large lima beans. Fava beans can be purchased dried, canned or fresh.

FLOWERS, EDIBLE: can be stored tightly wrapped in the refrigerator, up to a week. Some of the more popular edible flowers are the peppery-flavored nasturtiums, and chive blossoms, which taste like a mild, sweet onion. Pansies and violas offer a flavor of grapes. Some of the larger flowers such as squash blossoms can be stuffed and deep-fried.

FRISÉE: sweetest of the chicory family, with a mildly bitter taste. The leaves are a pale green, slender but curly.

FROMAGE BLANC CHEESE: fresh, day-old curds with some of the whey whipped back into the cheese. The texture is similar to ricotta cheese and is available plain or flavored.

GADO-GADO: this Indonesian favorite consists of a mixture of raw and slightly cooked vegetables served with a spicy peanut sauce.

GANACHE: a rich chocolate icing made of semisweet chocolate and whipping cream that are heated and stirred together until the chocolate has melted.

GNOCCHI: the Italian word for "dumplings," gnocchi are shaped into little balls, cooked in boiling water and served with butter and Parmesan or a savory sauce. The dough can also be chilled, sliced and either baked or fried.

GORGONZOLA CHEESE: a blue-veined Italian creamy cheese.

GRAHAM FLOUR: whole-wheat flour that is slightly coarser than the regular grind.

GRITS: coarsely ground grain such as corn, oats or rice. Grits can be cooked with water or milk by boiling or baking.

HABANERO CHILE: tiny, fat, neon orange-colored chiles that are hotter than the jalapeño chile.

HAZELNUT OIL: a lightly textured oil with a rich essence of hazelnut.

HUMMUS: this thick Middle Eastern sauce is made from mashed chickpeas seasoned with lemon juice, garlic and olive oil or sesame oil.

JALAPEÑO CHILE: these plump, thumb-size green chiles are known for wonderful flavor.

JICAMA: grows underground like a tuber, yet is part of the legume family. Beneath the thick brown skin, the flesh is creamy-white and sweet. Tastes like a cross between an apple and a potato.

KALAMATA OLIVES: intensely flavored, almond-shaped, dark purple Greek olives packed in brine.

KOSHER SALT: an additive-free, coarse-grained salt that is milder than sea salt.

LEMON GRASS: available in Asian food stores, this citrus-flavored herb has long, thin, gray-green leaves and a scallion-like base. Available fresh or dried.

LENTILS: the French or European lentil is grayish-brown with a creamy flavor. The reddish-orange Egyptian or red lentil is smaller and rounder. Lentils should be stored airtight at room temperature and will keep about 6 months. Lentils offer calcium and vitamins A and B, and are a good source of iron and phosphorus.

MÂCHE: also known as lamb's lettuce, has a delicate, sweet-nutty taste. The lettuce is a deep green.

MANGO: grows in a wide variety of shapes: oblong, kidney and round. Its thin, tough skin is green and, as the fruit ripens, becomes yellow with red mottling. Under-ripe fruit can be placed in a paper bag at room temperature.

MARJORAM: there are many species of this ancient herb, which is a member of the mint family. The most widely available is sweet marjoram or wild marjoram. Early Greeks wove marjoram into funeral wreaths and planted it on graves to symbolize their loved one's happiness, both in life and beyond.

MARSALA: a wine with a rich, smoky flavor that can range from sweet to dry.

MESCLUN: a traditional French mixture of tiny lettuces, including curly endive, red lettuce, Romaine, oak-leaf, butter lettuce and rocket.

MIRIN: a sweet cooking sake.

MISO: a fermented salty soybean paste made by crushing boiled soybeans with barley.

MOREL MUSHROOM: a wild mushroom that is cone-shaped with a spongy beige cap. Has a nutty taste.

NAPA CABBAGE: also known as Chinese cabbage, it looks like a cross between celery and lettuce, very much like romaine lettuce. The flavor is more delicate with a slight peppery taste.

NASTURTIUM FLOWERS: edible sweet and peppery flowers in a rainbow of colors. Nasturtiums are beautiful in salads and easy to grow.

NORI: paper-thin sheets of dried seaweed ranging in color from dark green to dark purple to black. Nori is rich in protein, vitamins, calcium, iron and other minerals.

OPAL BASIL: a beautiful purple basil with a pungent flavor.

OREGANO: this herb belongs to the mint family and is related to both marjoram and thyme, offering a strong, pungent flavor. Greek for "joy of the mountain," oregano was almost unheard of in the U.S. until soldiers came back from Italian World War II assignments raving about it.

OYSTER MUSHROOM: a beige fan-shaped wild mushroom with a mild flavor and soft texture.

PARMESAN CHEESE: a hard dry cheese made from skimmed or partially-skimmed cow's milk.

PECORINO CHEESE: a cheese made from sheep's milk

POLENTA: cornmeal—ground corn kernels, white or yellow, often enriched with butter and grated cheese. A staple of northern Italian cooking.

PORCINI MUSHROOM: parasol-shaped mushroom cap has a thick stem, with a meaty, smoky flavor.

QUINOA: served like rice or as a base for salads. Pale yellow in color and slightly larger than a mustard seed with a sweet flavor and soft texture.

RADICCHIO: this peppery-tasting lettuce with brilliant, ruby-colored leaves is available year-round, with a peak season from mid-winter to early spring. Choose heads that have crisp, full-colored leaves with no sign of browning. Store in a plastic bag in the refrigerator for up to a week.

RICE WINE VINEGAR: a light, clean-tasting vinegar that works perfectly as is, in salads, as well as in a variety of Asian-inspired dishes.

RISOTTO: an Italian rice specialty made by stirring hot stock in Arborio rice that has been sautéed in butter.

ROMAINE: known for a sweet nutty flavor, this lettuce has long, crisp, green or red leaves.

ROUX: a mixture of melted butter or oil and flour used to thicken sauces, soups and stews. Sprinkle flour into the melted, bubbling-hot butter, whisking constantly over low heat, cooking at least 2 minutes.

SAFFRON: a bright yellow, strongly aromatic spice that imparts a unique flavor. Store saffron in a cool dark place for up to 6 months.

SAVOY CABBAGE: also known as curly cabbage, has lacy leaves with a white or reddish trim.

SERRANO CHILE: a fat, squat, red or green hot chile. They are milder when roasted with the ribs and seeds removed.

SHIITAKE MUSHROOM: a Japanese mushroom sold fresh or dried, which imparts a distinctively rich flavor to any dish. The versatile shiitake is suitable for almost any cooking method including sautéing, broiling and baking.

SNOW PEAS: a translucent, bright green pod that is thin, crisp and entirely edible. The tiny seeds inside are tender and sweet. Snow peas are also called Chinese snow peas and sugar peas.

SORBET: a palate refresher between courses or as a dessert, the sorbet never contains milk and often has softer consistency than sherbet.

SOY MILK: higher in protein than cow's milk, this milky, iron-rich liquid is a non-dairy product made by pressing ground, cooked soybeans. Cholesterol-free and low in calcium, fat and sodium, it makes an excellent milk substitute.

SPAGHETTI SQUASH: a yellow watermelon-shaped squash whose flesh, when cooked, separates into spaghetti-like strands.

STRUDEL: a type of pastry made up of many layers of very thin dough spread with a filling, then rolled and baked until crisp.

SUN-DRIED TOMATOES: air-dried tomatoes sold in various forms such as marinated tomato halves, which are packed in olive oil, or a tapenade, which is puréed dried tomatoes in olive oil with garlic.

TAHINI: Middle Eastern in origin, tahini is made from crushed sesame seeds. Used mainly for its creamy, rich and nutty flavor as well as for binding food together.

TEMPEH: made from cultured, fermented soybeans; comes in flat, light, grainy-looking cakes.

TOFU: a versatile fresh soybean curd, tofu is an excellent and inexpensive form of protein. It is characteristically bland in taste, but can be enhanced with seasonings.

TOMATILLOS: green husk tomatoes; small with a tart, citrus-like flavor.

TRUFFLE: a fungus that grows underground near the roots of trees prized by gourmets for centuries. Truffles should be used as soon as possible after purchase, but can be stored up to 6 days in the refrigerator or for several months in the freezer. Canned truffles, truffle paste and frozen truffles can be found in specialty stores.

VIDALIA ONION: the namesake of Vidalia, Georgia where they thrive. This yellow onion, sweet and juicy, is available in the summer or by mail-order year-round.

WATERCRESS: this spicy-flavored green is dark in color with glossy leaves.

YUCCA: this root has a tough brown skin, which, when peeled, reveals a crisp, white flesh. Two main categories—sweet and bitter.

Mail Order Sources

If you are unable to locate some of the specialty food products used in *Florida's Cooking Secrets*, you can order them from the mail order sources listed below. These items are delivered by UPS, fully insured and at reasonable shipping costs.

DRIED BEANS AND PEAS

Baer's Best
154 Green Street
Reading, MA 01867
(617) 944-8719
Bulk or 1-pound packages of over 30 different varieties of beans, common to exotic. No peas.

The Bean Bag
818 Jefferson Street
Oakland, CA 94607
510-839-8988
Dried beans, including many heirloom and organic beans, and bean mixes; hot sauces; sun-dried tomatoes; gourmet rices, specialty grains.

Corti Brothers
5801 Folsom Blvd.
Sacramento, CA 95819
(916) 736-3800
Special gourmet items such as: imported extra-virgin olive oils, wines, exotic beans, egg pasta.

Dean & Deluca
560 Broadway
New York, NY 10012
(800) 221-7714
(212) 431-1691
Dried beans, salted capers, polenta, arborio rice, dried mushrooms, dried tomatoes, parmesan and reggiano cheeses, kitchen and baking equipment.

Phipps Ranch
P.O. Box 349
Pescadero, CA 94060
415-879-0787
Dried beans such as cannellini, cranberry, fava, flageolet, borlotti, scarlet runner, Tongues of Fire, and more. Also dried peas, herb vinegars, grains, herbs and spices.

DRIED MUSHROOMS

Den & Deluca
560 Broadway
New York, NY 10012
(800) 221-7714
(212) 431-1691
Dried beans, salted capers, polenta, arborio rice, dried mushrooms, dried tomatoes, parmesan and reggiano cheeses, kitchen and baking equipment.

G.B. Ratto & Co.
821 Washington St.
Oakland, CA 94607
(800) 325-3483
(510) 836-2250 fax
Imported pasta, dried beans, amaretti cookies, semolina flour, dried mushrooms, dried tomatoes, parmesan and reggiano cheeses.

Gold Mine Natural Food Co.
1947 30th St.
San Diego, CA 92102-1105
(800) 475-3663
Organic foods, dried foods, whole grain rice, Asian dried mushrooms, condiments, sweeteners, spices.

FLOURS AND GRAINS

Arrowhead Mills
Box 2059
Hereford, TX 79045
806-364-0730
A large variety of whole grain products, including specialty grains, grain mixes, flours, cereals.

Barbara's Bakery, Inc.
3900 Cypress Drive
Petaluma, CA 94954
707-765-2263
Whole grain and cereal products.

Butte Creek Mill

P.O. Box 561
Eagle Point, Oregon 97524
503-826-3531
A large assortment of cereals, whole grains, rolled grains, stone-ground flours and meals.

Continental Mills

P.O. Box 88176
Seattle, WA 98138
206-872-8400
Specialty whole grains, including bulgur.

Dean & Deluca

560 Broadway
New York, NY 10012
(800) 221-7714
(212) 431-1691
Dried beans, salted capers, polenta, arborio rice, dried mushrooms, dried tomatoes, parmesan and reggiano cheeses, kitchen and baking equipment.

G.B. Ratto & Co.

821 Washington Street
Oakland, CA 94607
(510) 832-6503
(800) 325-3483
Flours, rice, bulgar wheat, couscous, oils, and sun-dried tomatoes.

Gold Mine Natural Food Co.

1947 30th St.
San Diego, CA 92102-1105
(800) 475-3663
Organic foods, dried foods, whole grain rice, Asian dried mushrooms, condiments, sweeteners, spices.

King Arthur Flour Baker's Catalogue

P.O. Box 876
Norwich, VT 05055
(800) 827-6836
Semolina flour, all types of flours, wheat berries, kitchen and baking equipment.

Lundberg Family Farms

P.O. Box 369
Richvale, CA 95974-0369
916-882-4551
Premium short-grain and long-grain brown rice. California basmati brown rice, organic brown rice, specialty brown rices and rice blends, rice cakes and rice cereals.

Specialty Rice Marketing Inc.

P.O. Box 880
Brinkley, AR 72021
501-734-1234
Whole grains and cereals, including brown rice cereal.

U.S. Mills

4301 N. 30th Street
Omaha, NE 6811
402-451-4567
Whole grains and cereals, including brown rice cereals.

The Vermont Country Store

P.O. Box 3000
Manchester Center, VT 05255
(802) 362-2400 credit card
  orders
(802) 362-4647 customer
  service
Orders are taken 24 hours a day.
Many different varieties: whole wheat, sweet-cracked, stone-ground rye, buckwheat, cornmeal and many more. They also sell a variety of items which are made in Vermont.

FRUIT & VEGETABLES

Diamond Organics

Freedom, CA 95019
(800) 922-2396
Free catalog available. Fresh, organically grown fruits & vegetables, specialty greens, roots, sprouts, exotic fruits, citrus, wheat grass.

Giant Artichoke

11241 Merritt St.
Castroville, CA 95012
(408) 633-2778
Fresh baby artichokes.

Lee Anderson's Covalda Date Company

51-392 Harrison Street
  (Old Highway 86)
P.O. Box 908
Coachella, CA 92236-0908
(619) 398-3441
Organic dates, raw date sugar and other date products. Also dried fruits, nuts and seeds.

Northwest Select

14724 184th St. NE
Arlington, WA 98223
(800) 852-7132
(206) 435-8577
Fresh baby artichokes.

Timber Crest Farms

4791 Dry Creek Road
Healdsburg, CA 95448
(707) 433-8251
Domestic dried tomatoes and other unsulfured dried fruits and nuts.

SEEDS FOR GROWING HERBS AND VEGETABLES

Herb Gathering, Inc.
5742 Kenwood Ave.
Kansas City, MO 64110
(816) 523-2653
Seeds for growing herbs, fresh-cut herbs.

Shepherd's Garden Seeds
6116 Highway 9
Felton, CA 95018
(408) 335-6910
Excellent selection of vegetable and herb seeds with growing instructions.

The Cook's Garden
P.O. Box 535
Londonderry, VT 05148
(802) 824-3400
Organically grown, reasonably priced vegetable, herb and flower seeds. Illustrated catalog has growing tips and recipes.

Vermont Bean Seed Company
Garden Lane
Fair Haven VT 05743
(802) 273-3400
Selling over 60 different varieties of beans, peas, corn, tomato and flower seeds.

W. Atlee Burpee & Co.
Warminster, PA 18974
(800) 888-1447
Well-known, reliable, full-color seed catalog.

Well-Sweep Herb Farm
317 Mount Bethal Rd.
Port Murray, NJ 07865
(908) 852-5390
Seeds for growing herbs, fresh herb plants.

SPECIALTY FOODS AND FOOD GIFTS

China Moon Catalogue
639 Post St.
San Francisco, CA 94109
(415) 771-MOON (6666)
(415) 775-1409 fax
Chinese oils, peppers, teas, salts, beans, candied ginger, kitchen supplies, cookbooks.

Corti Brothers
5801 Folsom Blvd.
Sacramento, CA 95819
(916) 736-3800
Special gourmet items such as: imported extra-virgin olive oils, wines, exotic beans, egg pasta.

Festive Foods
9420 Arroyo Lane
Colorado Springs, CO 80908
(719) 495-2339
Spices and herbs, teas, oils, vinegars, chocolate and baking ingredients.

G.B. Ratto & Co.
821 Washington St.
Oakland, CA 94607
(800) 325-3483
(510) 836-2250 fax
Imported pasta, dried beans, amaretti cookies, semolina flour, dried mushrooms, dried tomatoes, parmesan and reggiano cheeses.

Gazin's Inc.
P.O. Box 19221
New Orleans, LA 70179
(504) 482-0302
Specializing in Cajun, Creole and New Orleans foods.

Gold Mine Natural Food Co.
1947 30th St.
San Diego, CA 92102-1105
(800) 475-3663
Organic foods, dried foods, whole grain rice, Asian dried mushrooms, condiments, sweeteners, spices.

Knott's Berry Farm
8039 Beach Boulevard
Buena Park, CA 90620
(800) 877-6887
(714) 827-1776
Eleven types of jams and preserves, nine of which are non-sugar.

Kozlowski Farms
5566 Gravenstein Highway
Forestville, CA 95436
(707) 887-1587
(800) 473-2767
Jams, jellies, barbecue and steak sauces, conserves, honeys, salsas, chutneys and mustards. Some products are non-sugared, others are in the organic line. You can customize your order from 65 different products.

Williams-Sonoma
Mail Order Dept.
P.O. Box 7456
San Francisco, CA 94120-7456
(800) 541-2233 credit card orders
(800) 541-1262 customer service
Vinegars, oils, foods and kitchenware.

SPICES AND HERBS

Apple Pie Farm, Inc. (The Herb Patch)
Union Hill Rd. #5
Malvern, PA 19355
(215)933-4215
A wide variety of fresh-cut herbs.

Festive Foods
9420 Arroyo Lane
Colorado Springs, CO 80908
(719) 495-2339
Spices and herbs, teas, oils, vinegars, chocolate and baking ingredients.

Fox Hill Farm
444 West Michigan Avenue
P.O. Box 9
Parma, MI 49269
(517) 531-3179
Fresh-cut herb plants, topiaries, ornamental and medicinal herbs.

Meadowbrook Herb Gardens
Route 138
Wyoming, RI 02898
(401) 539-7603
Organically grown herb seasonings, high quality spice and teas.

Nichols Garden Nursery
1190 N. Pacific Hwy.
Albany, OR 97321
(503) 928-9280
Fresh herb plants.

Old Southwest Trading Company
P.O. Box 7545
Albuquerque, NM 87194
(800) 748-2861
(505) 831-5144
Specializes in chiles, everything from dried chiles to canned chiles and other chile-related products.

Penzey Spice House Limited
P.O. Box 1633
Milwaukee, WI 53201
(414) 768-8799
Fresh ground spices (saffron, cinnamon and peppers), bulk spices, seeds, and seasoning mixes.

Rafal Spice Company
2521 Russell Street
Detroit, MI 48207
(800) 228-4276
(313) 259-6373
Seasoning mixtures, herbs, spices, oil, coffee beans and teas.

Spice Merchant
P.O. Box 524
Jackson Hole, WY 83001
(307) 733-7811
Specializes in Asian spices.

Recipe Index

About the Author

KATHLEEN DEVANNA FISH, author of the popular "Secrets" and "Pets Welcome™" series, is a gourmet cook and gardener who is always on the lookout for recipes with style and character.

In addition to *Florida's Cooking Secrets,* Kathleen has written *Cooking with the Masters of Food & Wine, The Elegant Martini, The Great California Cookbook, Great Vegetarian Cookbook, Cooking Secrets from America's South, Louisiana's Cooking Secrets, Pacific Northwest Cooking Secrets, Cooking Secrets for Healthy Living, The Gardener's Cookbook, California Wine Country Cooking Secrets, San Francisco's Cooking Secrets, Monterey's Cooking Secrets, New England's Cooking Secrets, Cape Cod's Cooking Secrets, Pets Welcome™ California, Pets Welcome™ America's South, Pets Welcome™ New England, Pets Welcome™ Southwest, Pets Welcome™ Pacific Northwest* and *Pets Welcome™ National.*

Before embarking on a writing and publishing career, she owned and operated three businesses in the travel and hospitality industry.

ROBERT FISH, award-winning photojournalist, produces the images that bring together the concept of the "Secrets" and "Pets™ Welcome" series.

In addition to taking the cover photographs, Robert explores the food and wine of each region, helping to develop the overview upon which each book is based.

Notes

Bon Vivant Press

A division of The Millennium Publishing Group

PO Box 1994 • Monterey, CA 93942

800-524-6826 • 831-373-0592 • FAX 831-373-3567 • http://www.millpub.com.

Send _____ copies of *Pets Welcome America's South* at $15.95 each.

Send _____ copies of *Pets Welcome California* at $15.95 each.

Send _____ copies of *Pets Welcome New England* at $15.95 each.

Send _____ copies of *Pets Welcome Pacific Northwest* at $15.95 each.

Send _____ copies of *Pets Welcome Southwest* at $15.95 each.

Send _____ copies of *Pets Welcome National Edition* at $19.95 each.

Add $4.50 postage and handling for the first book ordered and $1.50 for each additional book. Please add $1.08 sales tax per book, for those books shipped to California addresses.

Please charge my ☐ Visa   # _____
☐ MasterCard

Expiration date_____ Signature _____

Enclosed is my check for _____

Name _____

Address _____

City_____State_____Zip _____

☐ This is a gift. Send directly to:

Name _____

Address _____

City_____State_____Zip _____

☐ Autographed by the author
   Autographed to _____

Notes

Bon Vivant Press

A division of The Millennium Publishing Group

PO Box 1994 • Monterey, CA 93942

800-524-6826 • 831-373-0592 • FAX 831-373-3567 • http://www.millpub.com

Send _____ copies of *Cooking with the Masters of Food & Wine* at $34.95 each.

Send _____ copies of *Vegetarian Pleasures* at $19.95 each.

Send _____ copies of *The Elegant Martini* at $17.95 each.

Send _____ copies of *Florida's Cooking Secrets* at $15.95 each.

Send _____ copies of *Cooking Secrets from Around the World* at $15.95 each.

Send _____ copies of *Cooking Secrets from America's South* at $15.95 each.

Send _____ copies of *Louisiana's Cooking Secrets* at $15.95 each.

Send _____ copies of *Pacific Northwest Cooking Secrets* at $15.95 each.

Send _____ copies of *Cooking Secrets for Healthy Living* at $15.95 each.

Send _____ copies of *The Great California Cookbook* at $15.95 each.

Send _____ copies of *The Gardener's Cookbook* at $15.95 each.

Send _____ copies of *The Great Vegetarian Cookbook* at $15.95 each.

Send _____ copies of *California Wine Country Cooking Secrets* at $14.95 each.

Send _____ copies of *San Francisco's Cooking Secrets* at $13.95 each.

Send _____ copies of *Monterey's Cooking Secrets* at $13.95 each.

Send _____ copies of *New England's Cooking Secrets* at $14.95 each.

Send _____ copies of *Cape Cod's Cooking Secrets* at $14.95 each.

Send _____ copies of *Jewish Cooking Secrets From Here and Far* at $14.95 each.

Add $4.50 postage and handling for the first book ordered and $1.50 for each additional book. Please add $1.08 sales tax per book, for those books shipped to California addresses.

Please charge my ☐ Visa # _____
              ☐ MasterCard

           Expiration date_____Signature _____

Enclosed is my check for _____

Name _____

Address _____

City_____State_____Zip _____

☐ This is a gift. Send directly to:

Name _____

Address _____

City_____State_____Zip _____

☐ Autographed by the author
   Autographed to _____

Notes